THE CANVAS OF GREEN

AWADHESH K OJHA

INDIA • SINGAPORE • MALAYSIA

ISBN

Hardcase 979-8-89544-859-5
Paperback 979-8-89322-953-0

At birth, your life was a plain canvas.
Your potential is the colours.
Your Choices are the strokes on the canvas.

At death, this canvas
will either be a treasured masterpiece
or an unnoticed scribbling.

That would be the judgment day
on how good a painter you were
in painting your life.

– Mahatria Ra

Dedication

To my father, who, by holding my fingers, taught me to walk, run, and conquer the ups and downs of life.

To my wife, with her innocence, immense value system, and support – without her, the story of learning and success would not have been possible.

To my children, from whom I learn more than what they learn from me.

And to my grandchildren, who make me relive my childhood days once again…

Contents

Acknowledgment

This book is my humble tribute to the spirit of Tatas – a group where I spent my entire career – and to colleagues, friends, and family who stood by me when I needed them the most.

This book also belongs to those who knowingly or unknowingly became my mentors or coaches and helped me grow in life and career.

People talk about the power of 'one.' I experienced it as I joined and superannuated from the same company after four decades. Words will fall short for me to express my feelings and gratitude for the company which gave me everything; and the most important thing which it gave me was my identity.

Yes, Tata Steel has become my identity. It gives me pride and a sense of fulfillment even after having superannuated from the group. Some of my best friends are still those who worked with me and from whom I learned so much that I can never repay their love and kindness. All that I can feel is an unmistakable sense of gratitude.

I am grateful for the trust bestowed upon me by Mr. B Muthuraman, the then MD and subsequently the

Vice Chairman of Tata Steel. At a time in my career when I felt like stagnating, I was given the role of the Head of the division where I started my career as a Graduate Trainee. The roles, responsibilities, and challenges which came along proved to be the icing on the cake as I said adieu to the company on my superannuation. Some of the crucial leadership lessons included in the book would not have been feasible without the belief and support of Mr. Muthuraman.

I received a lot of support and guidance from Dr. T Mukherjee as I took over the role of head of one of the most crucial raw material divisions. The achievements which I made – however small these might be in the overall scheme of things for a massive organization like Tata Steel Limited – were not feasible without the mentoring and support of Dr. Mukherjee. He encouraged and supported us in our endeavor to lower the ash % and achieve 13 months production in 12 months. I owe him a lot in my journey as a person and professional.

Mr. A D Baijal was not only my superior, but he was also a mentor. Those who know him may remember him as a strict disciplinarian, but I was privileged to see beneath a tough personality, a boss who truly cared for his people, wanted them to grow in life and career, and supported them by often going out of the way.

Mr. A M Misra was not only a superior who inspired me and other colleagues to aim for bigger goals and achieve more, but he was also a true professional and life mentor. I still remember how one evening he came to my place and gifted me a motivational book authored by Mr. Pramod Batra. I read the book later and still remember some of the lessons which have helped me a lot in my career and life. He brought a renewed sense of pride and joy for all of us while working at West Bokaro, and I am sure many of my colleagues, having spent some golden years of their life and career at West Bokaro would share my feelings. The place became a shinier, happier, and more productive division with him coming to be with us for a few years.

I have made a few mentions of my enriching association with Mr. R N Sharma, known for his simplicity and thorough professionalism. We were fortunate to be in contact with Mr. Sharma during my career path in the mid-1980s. He was placed as the Head of the Raw Material Division. I learned from him the attitudes and attributes of a good professional and praiseworthy human being. Later on, when I superannuated from the company and settled in Jamshedpur, I was privileged to be associated with him once again during my times at the golf course. In this new phase of my life, it was all about yoga lessons and interaction with different personalities of different talents, acumen, attributes, and preferences. Mr. Sharma was more importantly a father figure for me, available for any turbulence of time.

The Law of Attraction says that sooner or later, we start seeing people who work with us to convert our dreams into reality. Arun Singh has worked closely with me to ensure that my dream book, which was in my mind, comes to fruition.

I thank Kavya, Kamal and team from Notion Press for working tirelessly and ensuring that the book is released on time and is easily available for people to order their copies.

Last but not least, I thank all the readers without whom the book means nothing. Thank you so much for holding a copy of the book, and I do hope that this book will bring more success and joy into your life and career.

That is all I have kept in mind while writing this book, which is meant only for you.

– Awadhesh K Ojha
Noida
9th June 2024

Foreword

Mr. AK Ojha and I were contemporaries working for the same company - Tata Steel, but were separated by the workplace - I worked in the Steel Plant at Jamshedpur and he at the Coal Mines at West Bokaro. However, we were destined to work together closely when I was transferred to West Bokaro colliery in 2002 as the General Manager. Being new to the colliery, I had to lean on my senior colleagues for guidance. Though Mr. Ojha had started his career as a mechanical engineer responsible for the maintenance of Heavy Earth Moving Machineries, he had developed an excellent understanding of mine planning which he utilized in increasing the productivity of the mine. While attempting to implement new initiatives, I found in Mr. Ojha a willingness to reflect and experiment with these newer ideas for the benefit of the company. As the Chief of Quarry, he displayed tremendous drive and readiness to accept challenges. He would successfully motivate his team to achieve stretched targets. Subsequently, he rose up in the organization and took over the mantle of General Manager after I moved back to Jamshedpur - the people and the division thrived under his leadership. We have remained in close association ever since.

Mr. Ojha is also a keen sportsman. He loved playing Cricket and after retirement has taken to playing golf, and I would meet him often on the course. It is remarkable how quickly he has improved his score – a reflection of his love for the game.

Another facet of Mr. Ojha's personality is his zest for life and adventure. I am glad that he has decided to pen down the stories from his life, reflecting his attitude, his willingness to learn and adapt. I recall I had once presented him a self-help book by Dr. Pramod Batra, which he finished in no time and was ever eager to engage with me in discussion.

It is now his turn to publish a book recounting his reflections on life, emphasizing that in ever-changing times, the recipe for success has remained the same. Our cultural ethos places great value on transmitting knowledge from one generation to another. In this regard, I am sure this book would be a valuable gift for the younger generation who aspire to fulfill higher goals in life.

I hope Mr. Ojha continues to write more books for the benefit of society.

– A M Misra

Former Vice President, Tata Steel,
& Former Chairman, Tata Sponge

Preface

Life is challenging. It's a lifelong battle to first build and then to ensure that things do not slip back while working hard to let our achievements grow further. Again, life consists of peaks and valleys, and there is no guarantee that after you have climbed a peak of fulfillment and greatness, you won't find yourself in the valleys of despair and hopelessness. But, broadly speaking, we can surely keep getting more success and higher peaks.

One factor which I have seen making life especially intriguing and tough is the fact that we all do not begin from the same starting point. Unlike in a race, we all start from different points. Some of us start from a long distance behind and some others start from a vantage point. In other words, we all are not born with the same set of resources. Some of us are born to rich parents in a mansion overlooking a fleet of high-end cars and others are born in slums to parents who do not even have a proper house to live in and hygienic food to eat.

In between, there are crores of families who are born, live and die an average life.

Let me narrate an experience here. I have once gone on a trekking expedition and have also seen my children going on a few. On such a trek, the participants must often cook their food. People are segregated into different groups and each group is given the same ration of grains, vegetables, and pulses. But every group will invariably cook a different recipe of different taste from the same set of ingredients.

In life, it's even more complex as we all get different ingredients. It's all up to us what kind of recipe we prepare from it. Life is what you make it.

What makes living truly interesting is – our starting point does not define the ultimate life which we can create. There are CEOs rising from an impoverished background and stories of failures coming out of sky-kissing palaces.

All that we can say is – life is a gift from God. We must accept whatever we have got and work continuously to build the castles of our dreams. We must perform our duties, and that is the only thing in our hands.

I was born in a village without even a basic school and had every reason to crib and complain.

Today, I consider myself blessed and privileged to fund the construction of a modern high school in the same village.

The journey in between is encapsulated in this book.

This book has an encapsulating story of my travel from a small village to Jamshedpur and from there to West Bokaro before traveling across many other countries while working with some of the best brains in the world and learning a lot of lessons on the way. I want to share these with the youth hoping that some of these will make sense to them and will help them run their own race of life successfully. Let the world be a better place to live, love, laugh, and work.

Introduction

We are at the cusp of a major change in the way we are living and working. It's a world of distractions primarily due to the invasion of social media in all aspects of life. The youth of today wants everything at their beck and call. Artificial Intelligence has made any kind of information possible within a few seconds in the way you desire. AI tools like ChatGPT can do many tasks better and faster than human beings, and it has already started replacing people in certain areas. OTT channels have started providing endless entertainment and even a one-minute reel on social media must compete with millions of reels for the attention of the viewer.

The first casualty of such a 'speedy' and 'fast-changing world' is a set of core values and success factors which were, are, and will always remain important for the success of anyone and everyone. Qualities like Focus, Discipline, Concentration, Persistence, Patience, Hard Work, Commitment, Dedication, and Resilience are being forgotten or given less importance.

There is a difference between *vidya* and *shiksha*. You can attain shiksha in schools but vidya can be attained only by observing life and reflecting on our experiences.

This book is about *vidya* for which there is no word in English.

The fact is – these qualities were, are, and will remain at the core of any worthwhile success ever attained by any human being. And hence, I thought of writing this book.

The book narrates my true story while working with some very inspiring people for decades, with nuggets of lessons that will hopefully pave the path of the youth toward a better tomorrow. It contains inspiring lessons on parenting, learning, work, relationships, joys, fulfillment, and success while building on all the time-tested human qualities which are needed even more today.

The eight laws of power which I learned in an all-India-one training institute many decades ago are even relevant today. I worked with a few very powerful leaders and learned lessons on how to inspire teams and channel their energy in one direction. There is a chapter dedicated to this. There are chapters talking about the power of Visionary leadership. "Vision without action is merely a dream. Action without vision just passes the time. Vision with action can change the world." Said Joel A Barker. I have shared my personal experience on this subject.

Also, there are chapters on the 'care' which you need to take to stay safe against people who may drive you in the wrong way.

To encapsulate the summary in a few words – it's a book which will talk about all that you should know and practice and the things which you should keep away from. And what I have mentioned above is not even the tip of the iceberg! Discover the joy of reading yourself.

Thank you for laying your hands on the book.

CHAPTER ONE

Many Colors of Life

Every color has many shades.

But no other color fascinates me as deeply as the colors of yellow and orange.

Being an early morning riser, I have always enjoyed noticing a new shade of yellow or orange on the horizon in the sky.

As the darkness of the night gives way to the early morning shine, nature paints the canvas of the sky with different shades.

Yellow. Amber. Copper. Golden. Saffron. Lemon yellow. Canary yellow. Mustard. Etc.

Then I have noticed the full family in orange. Orange-red. Vivid orange. Pumpkin orange, etc.

I have noticed all of these and more in the brushstrokes of nature in the early morning hours.

I am always fascinated with these hues and shades of refreshing and energetic colors, and this is one of the many temptations for me to wake up early.

It's the time when it's dark outside when I get up. The alarm clock is set for early morning hours for me and it has been like that for many years.

No, I think it has been that way for decades, in fact. My habits are close to my heart and some exercise and yoga in the morning hours has been a constant in my life for decades.

I am 72 now but these habits have kept me young.

But then I think – these habits are not the only constants in my life.

There is another thing which I have lived with since my early childhood days.

Sports has been a way of life for me. I have worked closely with youngsters for many decades during my corporate life and have always advised them on one thing – to include some form of sports in their life.

Forever. Till they Live.

Though I have been playing many forms of sports, there is one very close to my heart.

It gives me a reason to wake up early, especially on the weekends.

When I came to Noida, the first thing I did was to look for a nearby golf course. Some wise man had said – you see what you want to see. While many people, upon coming to Noida, might be searching for nearby eating joints, multiplexes, and malls, I searched for golf courses. I found many. Jaypee Green golf Course, Unitech golf Course, Noida golf Course and more. I immediately got enrolled in one and it has been a part of my life since then.

I get ready and come out where the chauffeur is waiting for me. As I leave for the golf course, the sky is colored with the hues of white and yellow. It's sunrise time and the traffic snarls are yet to build up. I always like driving in the early morning hours for the fresh breeze, early sunshine, and lean traffic.

Through the windows, I see the tall and multi-story buildings which surround the road from both sides.

While my love for the green grass on the golf course has remained the same over decades, many things have changed. And no, I am not talking about my age or gray and white hairs. I have always felt young at heart and have surrounded myself with people who feel even younger than me. Hence, I feel like the same youth I used to be decades ago, well, almost like the same.

The youth that I used to be in the place which gave me so much. I owe most of my sweet memories and experiences to this place.

The place which surely was different from Noida.

This is a big change in my life.

I played my first game of golf in Jamshedpur where buildings were short in height but sprawling in size.

Noida is a vertical city. Jamshedpur was known for its horizontal spread. Large gardens in front of the house, wide roads, huge lakes, orchards and parks and many large golf courses.

I still remember my first day on the golf course in Jamshedpur.

Or, better, before I talk about my tryst with golf, let me begin from the beginning.

As I narrate my story, I will keep sharing a few learnings which I am sure will guide the youth and elderly alike.

I wrote about different shades of colors in the morning sky at the beginning of this chapter.

This book is also about different shades of life and emotions. Yes, emotions also have different shades. Happiness, for example, has different colors of joys, excitement, gratitude, contentment, etc.

This book is about the different emotions of life, and I am sure you would connect with many of these.

This book is also about different colors of learnings and life lessons. I am sure you will find these coming in time.

You don't have to spend decades getting some of these life lessons. You will get these in the book and hopefully, like a torch, the book will pave your path ahead in your life and career.

After all, though the book is my story, the goal is not to tell you my story. The aim is to help readers be a healthier, happier, and stronger version of themselves by reading a book that will both entertain and inspire them. It will inspire you to do what is right and not to do what should not be done, although I did some of these only to learn some vital lessons. I have written this book to share some crucial learnings so that the readers take some steps proactively and lead a happier, more successful, and fulfilling life.

"As you move to the next chapter, I would encourage you to make some reflections on your life, career, success stories, challenges, moments of glory, and moments which taught you lessons that shaped you into a better human being.

It is through reflections that we learn from our experiences and that of others.

It is through reflections that you experience the true beauty of life and the universe.

That is what Steve Jobs meant when he said – you can connect the dots only when you look back..."

CHAPTER TWO

One Step of Courage

I spent my childhood days in the beautiful city of Jamshedpur. I studied there in a good school. The place has a good number of sports grounds, and I had a lovely time playing and honing my skills in one form of the sports or the other. The place today is known as a great place to live with many gardens, parks, playgrounds, schools, shopping areas, good roads, and health care centers. Of course, all of this is there due to one name – Tata. This globally respected group has one of the largest facilities for producing steel and cars here. Apart from Tata Steel and Tata Motors, there are other Tata Companies as well in Jamshedpur. There are hundreds of subsidiary and OEM Companies in and around the city of Jamshedpur. The place provides a great source of earning, living, and enjoying life and work.

There are beautiful clubs and golf courses. One can choose which club to get the membership of. There are many golf courses, and one can also choose which golf course to go to enjoy the weekend morning hours. Nice eateries and snack centers are galore, and all festivals are celebrated here with fervor and enthusiasm. You have beautiful roads to drive through and sports stadiums to go for your morning jog and to watch events and sports.

People here live with love and peace, and everyone seeks great pride in offering deep respect to the founder of the Tata group – Mr Jamshedji Nusserwanji Tata on 3rd March every year.

Of course, today we have more facilities in the form of new malls and shopping areas, but even in the years I spent my childhood days in the place, it was no less beautiful. With fewer concrete structures and more natural habitat, I have vivid memories of beautiful years spent at the place.

Today, I always feel grateful to my father who took the first step of courage to come out of our village in Bihar and settle in Jamshedpur. He was the only brother in his generation to have come out of the village. All my cousin brothers spent their life in villages while following the family tradition of doing farming and other related work which people had been doing for decades. Farming is a respected profession, but they could never get the kind of support and facilities which I was privy to. Good education, electricity, quality of life, and sports – I could enjoy all of these because my father himself decided to walk all the way for miles every day to do his schooling at a time the village did not have any school and the nearest school demanded one to walk for hours, one way.

My father had great inquisitiveness about education. He channeled his energy for getting a good education in the 1930s and succeeded till the school level. That itself was a challenging phase. Thereafter, it was not a good and easy proposition to establish himself in the industry and farming. He was waiting for an opportunity to be available in the pre-independence era and he subsequently got this opportunity at Jamshedpur.

Today, when my son is traveling across the globe and my daughter is settled in the USA, I know it's all because of my father who was the first to get educated and secure a job in a great city.

It's not only because of me.

When one person decides to take a step of courage out of the village either for education or for a job, it's a mega leap for the forthcoming generations. All forthcoming generations are transformed for great reasons.

It's time for reflection on your own life and career decisions.

When was the last time you took a step with courage and did what you thought was right? One step of courage will teach you more about life than dozens of books ever can. Anything worthwhile which anyone has ever done is coming out of the seed of courage. When you strongly believe in something right, be polite but also be courageous. Most people will tell you to compromise in life and give up on your original ideas even if you know these are right. They would ask you not to rock the boat and maintain a low profile. While you do so, always believe that life becomes better not because of 'compromises' but because of 'acts of courage.'

Many people talk about the power of contributing to society.

In my opinion, one act of courage would do more good for society than any act of charity.

One step of courage by my father did the same for me and my family.

"Let us take steps of courage when needed and not be limited by our comfort zones of 'perceived security.' We may not change the world, but we may certainly make a worthy change in our lives as well as in the lives of future generations. Not one action of courage taken with the right intention goes in vain. It manifests in some outcome, somewhere, at some point in time."

CHAPTER THREE

The Boy from the Village

Let me share a bit about my early days in the village. That's where the earliest memories of my life started taking shape.

"A feeling of great pleasure or happiness that comes from success, good fortune, or a sense of well-being" – this is how people define joy.

In different phases of life, the source of joy keeps changing.

But there are certain moments that will always remain etched in my memory.

Some of these moments come from my childhood days.

I can't think of my childhood days in Jamshedpur without thinking of the joy of anticipating annual summer vacations. And it was not only to get some free time from the busy school routine. It was also because of the annual trip to our village.

I loved going to the village every year, and we loved just everything about this annual ritual. In fact, it was not a mere ritual for us. It was an event we used to look forward to. Initially, I used to go with family, but after graduating to class eight, I was also allowed to go with my cousin brother. I started enjoying my trips with my cousin as that allowed us greater freedom.

The fun used to begin with the travel itself. In those days, we had an evening train from Jamshedpur which used to take us to Patna. I am talking about the early 1960s when there was no system for reservation of berths except in the first-class compartments. In second, third, or general class, one just had to buy tickets and board the train by occupying whichever seat one found vacant. Finding a berth was not an easy task. Much before we started reading idioms like 'an early bird catches the prey,' we practiced this for grabbing a berth until Patna.

This meant we had to be early – at least three hours before the train was to leave Jamshedpur station – and head straight to the shunting yard where the bogies or coaches of the train were usually parked. We thought we were really early, but we always found some other people already occupying a few of the berths. I must say, getting a seat was usually a pretty adventurous experience; and a humbling one too! Humbling because no matter how early we reached the station and boarded the stationary train, some 'earlier birds were always there having caught the prey (read berths)' and welcoming us with an unmistakable sense of pride!

We used to sit doing nothing in the coach for a few hours before the train started moving, lurching slowly to the platform. That was usually half an hour before the time of departure. Now, it was our time to get alert and keep occupying our full seat in an authoritarian style as people started rushing inside the train even as it was still slowing down and had not come to a complete halt. Soon, it was like people running from all sides looking for their seat. They came through doors as well as windows. More athletic or adventurous ones used to jump inside through emergency windows and used to keep some seats 'reserved' for others by placing their handkerchiefs on the berths. The less adventurous ones entered through the regular doors and ran helter-skelter looking for an empty seat.

Now it was our turn to feel the sense of pride while occupying our seats, which was nothing less than 'defending our territories.' Our three hours of waiting on the berth in the shunting yard was worth it as the train left, and we, after having our dinner, slept comfortably in the train. But often, due to heavier rush, we failed to get a full seat (mostly on upper levels) and used to share the seat with others. But still, we considered ourselves lucky to have a sitting or resting place.

After some time, the train started moving, and people started opening their bags to take out their evening snacks. Some of them shared their snacks with others, and others ate without even recognizing that others who sat right across them. Some of them started making temporary friends while chatting on a range of topics including politics, movies, and the condition of Indian Railways. Some others kept looking outside the windows as if there was nothing inside the coaches for them. Or maybe they just wanted to make the best of their window seats, which was a privilege only for those who came well in advance to board the bogeys in the shunting yards.

"India is a country of unity in diversity" – we had read this in schoolbooks, but a train journey was a 'practical' of the 'theory' which we learned in the textbooks. To me, it was a human laboratory where I saw different human beings displaying different behaviors.

A train journey also provided ample opportunities to learn an important life lesson – You should and can have fun even in the most challenging situations. We enjoyed our journey even while being in a somewhat challenging situation.

We used to wake up in the early morning hours as the train approached Patna, still about half an hour away. Many vendors rushed with packets of breakfast to the windows as the train reached *Barhiya* railway station. The smell and look of Puris, Sabji, and Jalebi provided enough temptation to sit up on the berths and get ready by winding up our luggage to get down at the upcoming Patna junction.

Getting up was also important as around the same time, some women laborers used to board the train and asked us in rough – and often an authoritarian voice – to get up and sit straight so that they also could occupy some portion of the berth.

It was the onset of morning marking the beginning of a more crowded phase of our journey which was about to come.

We used to come out of the train, rubbing sleep from our eyes, and step down onto the ever-busy Patna railway station. From there, we would take horse carts or buggies (called 'tam-tam' in the local language) primarily because of the sound created by ringing bells tied to the horses' necks and the movements of metal parts of the cart, to reach the bank of the River Ganges. Now, it was time for us to board a steamer boat from Mahendru Ghat, which was situated on the bank of the river. During those years, there was no bridge over the River Ganges. The Mahatma Gandhi Setu – one of the largest river-bridges in the world – was constructed much later in 1982. I am narrating the events of the late 1960s when steamer boats were the only means of crossing the river that horizontally bifurcated the state of Bihar into two parts.

We would cross to the other side of the river while enjoying the sight of waves splashing away from the steamer ship or boat. A bus was the next mode of transportation that would take us to a town near our village. From there, we would take a smaller bus, and this was how we reached our village.

It was a long journey of almost 18 hours, but the train ride, steamer crossing, and bus trips were filled with fun.

In the village, it was a gala time – free, natural, and full of village games and trips to nearby villages to meet relatives. These were the peak months of summer season, which meant that the orchards in the village were laden with mangoes of different types, colors, and tastes. We would often spend our days in the mango groves, eating unripe mangoes with salt and red chili powder, and testing each other on our knowledge of math, science, and general knowledge. Village students of my age would often ask me questions to show that they were also good students despite being from a village. In fact, some of them were quite talented. We also searched for ripe mangoes on trees, and spotting one at an approachable height would fill us with joy. We played different games in the cool shade of the trees.

Occasionally, we played football in the playground of the only village school, which was available due to the summer vacation and was welcoming for us during the holidays.

In later years of my visits to the village, my sisters and cousins were married in nearby villages, and I often traveled to these villages to meet them. Each village had a distinct look and feel, and it was a lovely experience to visit both nearby and more distant ones and meet relatives. I was always treated like a king at my sisters' houses and got to eat homemade delicacies. Though as per prevailing social etiquettes, you are not expected to admit it too often, I always enjoyed the food there. It's always better to be repeatedly requested or forced to eat rather than asking for the food yourself. This is on a lighter note, but anyone coming from that background knows what I mean.

On other days, we used to go swimming in the nearby river. Children loved pushing each other into the shallow end of the river and jumping into the streams. It was one of the coolest ways of beating the summer heat and having some fun. The charm of jumping and swimming in the river water in those days would easily surpass the fun that today's children have in ultra-modern water theme parks. I remember my initial days of learning to swim; it was always with a sense of fear until someone pushed me from behind, and I fell into the shallow water—that's how I learned to swim.

A push is often all that you need to make new discoveries and learn new lessons in life. I did not know it then but realized it later.

Coming from a city as well-known as Jamshedpur, we were always seen with respect—and often with a bit of envy—by the village children and elderly people. They also used to test us on our knowledge of subjects. I often noticed how healthy a lifestyle the villagers used to maintain. By eight or nine at night, everyone was asleep. The village turned silent early in the night, and people started waking up around four in the morning.

This strict 'early to bed and early to rise' routine was not new for me, as my father always used to wake us up early in the morning even in Jamshedpur. Hence, the village routine was nothing new for us.

Out of the five hundred houses in the village, at least one family member from around a hundred houses had migrated to some other city or town to work and earn a livelihood. People from other houses were farmers. The houses from where a family member had migrated to outside cities or towns looked better kept and maintained. These houses appeared painted and equipped with more amenities like a hand pump for clean drinking water and a boundary wall for safety. These were pucca houses with a proper roof and many rooms. There used to be a visitors' sitting area outside the house.

Our house was one of the most prominent ones in the village. There was a courtyard outside the house to host visitors who used to visit often. Later, my father also funded the construction of a school building in the village. Being from a well-recognized and respected house had its own rewards. People used to welcome us and treat us well.

An unwavering focus on education always brought respect to our family. My father was one of the very few youngsters from the village to have continued his studies and secure a good job later. My grandfather also had education up to secondary school.

Hence, education was always an 'in-thing' for us, and we were always serious about studies and securing good grades in school. I still remember how my father used to wake us up for our studies at around 5-5:30 in the morning before himself getting ready and leaving for work in Jamshedpur.

So why did I narrate the story of my village here? It's with a certain intention.

I do not see the same urge among the current generation of people to visit villages and spend some cool time in the lap of nature while mingling with extended family members. It's my heartiest wish to do something to ensure that my children, and even their children, visit villages occasionally and stay connected to their roots. One of the things which I have been doing is to provide good amenities like AC, etc., in our village house so that the coming generations do not feel the lack of amenities and they are at ease while visiting villages. Once every few months – and certainly more than once every year – I visit my village and spend a few days while developing the house and adding some amenities with one goal – I do not want my coming generations to lose connect with their roots from where it all started.

Staying connected to your roots is important. It tells you the story of where the journey started from and keeps you grounded and strong in the ups and downs of life. In my opinion, a person who uproots himself from his cultural and family fabric does not experience a wholesome life. I am not alone in thinking so. I have many South Indian friends and colleagues and know how deeply rooted they are in their ancestral houses and village culture. This is true of people from almost all parts of the country. A tree can reach any height until it is firmly rooted in the ground. Similarly, a person can attain any height of success until he does not forget his family values.

"The reason behind telling you the story of my village days, however insignificant it might appear, is to share just one message with you all – Do not lose contact with your family members, childhood friends, mentors, and teachers. A life lived with old connections and people who love you is a life lived well. In a world of social media as well, things are not going to change a lot, and real, long, and deep connections are always going to remain relevant and, in fact, will gain even more significance.

Basic foundations of living a happy life are always going to remain the same."

CHAPTER FOUR

A Beautiful City

> "Be sure to lay wide streets planted with shady trees, every other of a quick-growing variety. Be sure that there is plenty of space for lawns and gardens. Reserve large areas for football, hockey, and parks. Earmark areas for Hindu temples, Mohammedan mosques, and Christian churches."
>
> **– J N Tata**

No other corporate house in India has set up a township as an integral part of their business strategy as beautifully and effectively as Tata has.

I see many organizations today setting up factories and arranging houses and other amenities for their employees.

Tata group Companies – for example, Tata Steel Limited – are not only profit-making organizations; these companies have also been contributing toward building the surrounding community.

In my opinion, Tata Steel does not only build steel; it also builds the nation. And surely it builds beautifully planned towns where people love to work and live safely and joyfully with their families.

I spent my childhood days in the city of Jamshedpur and can say so from my personal experience.

Reflecting on my childhood days in the 1960s – it has been almost 60 years since then – I can still remember how the company had a separate department for providing quality education to employees' children. Even today, you can hardly think of companies that will consider giving employment to employees' children. The focus of most companies lies in making a profit.

This shows there will never be a time, even in the far future, when any other company can get even close to the way of working of Tatas toward building societies and countries. There is a reason why people say Tata is not a group; it is a timeless institution.

I remember how even in the 1960s, Tata Steel had separate departments for providing good houses, making roads and parks, providing water and power, extending medical care, and building good schools for the proper education of employees' children.

I can recall the days during my studies from primary to higher secondary school while being in Jamshedpur.

During those years, most of the schools were monitored and maintained by Tata Steel, and there were hardly any good private schools. I used to attend one of the schools managed by Tata Steel and could easily see the difference in the quality of infrastructure and education between Tata-managed schools and government-run schools in villages. There were a few primary schools after which, based on their marks, students graduated to the middle schools. These were not exactly English medium schools but were 'English biased' schools.

'English biased' means most of the subjects related to Science (Physics, Chemistry, Maths, etc.) were taught in English, though there was no restriction for people to speak in English on the campus. Other subjects were taught in Hindi. In other words, chemistry was still chemistry; it was not *Rasayan Shashtra*, and Physics was Physics, not *Bhautik Vigyan*. It may also be compared with a *Hinglish* (Hindi + English) way of teaching.

Some of the schools which I can think of from those days were KMPM, R D Tata School, DM Madam Girls School, and Workers' College. The best students used to converge in two higher secondary schools, i.e., KMPM and R D Tata School. On the road down Basant Talkies, there was a Co-Operative college for boys and girls. All these were managed by Tatas. As far as the quality of education was concerned, students did not lack in any dimension compared to students from other parts of the world. Even in the 1950s-60s, government agencies from the field of education and local leaders used to appreciate Tata's efforts to educate children at par with the best in the country.

This legacy continues.

Today, everyone is aware that 3rd March is celebrated as The Founders' Day in Jamshedpur. The celebration started somewhere during the 1950s. I remember, on 3rd March every year, we used to reach our school early in the morning. We used to get up by 5 AM, get ready and be in the school by 5:45 AM. Then we used to march toward the main entrance of Tata Steel where we offered flowers to the statue and got a packet of sweets. That is how the celebrations started, which today has become a grand occasion in the city when the entire city is decorated like a new bride. Jubilee Park is illuminated so well that families come in the evening to get enthralled with the decoration.

There were no school buses until the early 1960s. We used to ride bicycles. I used to ride along with my brother in a 'one and a half pedal' way (the second person sitting on the front horizontal rod of the bicycle also pedals down). In case there was an issue with the bicycle (chain going down or a breakdown taking place), we had to run and walk intermittently to be at school on time. Sometimes, we were given money to take a bus. We would board the bus, and the conductor would not charge us. He was supportive as he knew we would use the money to buy some chocolates or snacks in school.

There was a high level of discipline maintained in the school where I studied. All students were expected to come in neat uniforms with all buttons properly tucked in. If someone came in unbuttoned shirts, they were questioned. Classes were held as per the regular schedule, and examinations were conducted according to the annual calendar.

I remember the day when Jawaharlal Nehru came to Jamshedpur to inaugurate the Jubilee Park. We were standing beside the road and saw Pandit Nehru being driven in an open car. We threw garlands of flowers toward him.

My father often used to have conversations with us, telling us about important happenings in Tata Steel and elsewhere. While hearing some of the stories, I gained insight that if you decide as an organizational leader to contribute to society in all fields of education, health, entertainment, etc., the workers will pay you back handsomely. I say so because there was a strike in 1956-57 which went on for a month. A few workers stayed in the factory even beyond their shifts for days together to ensure that the factory did not stop. My father used to narrate some of these stories with a sense of pride about the company.

Talking about the healthcare system, I remember every colony had a primary healthcare center known as a Dispensary. These had minimum facilities available with a doctor sitting there during the daytime for primary check-ups. In case of serious health matters or emergencies, patients were recommended to Tata Main Hospital (TMH). It was a 'hub and spoke' model in healthcare where TMH was the 'hub' and Dispensaries were the 'spokes.' When I hear some politicians talking nowadays about 'Mohalla clinics' (meaning 'neighborhood clinics,' we are not sure about the implementation of this project though), I know how Tatas had these arrangements well in place many decades ago without even talking about them. It shows the mighty character of this great business house.

Jamshedpur has always been a green city with a lot of flora and fauna around. Jubilee Park is just one example. When the company was developing the city, it did not cut Sal trees (a deciduous tree which is tall in height and wide in trunk diameter) which were in abundance in the area. These trees were still there in the courtyards. There were parks and gardens. We had fun playing in the green areas around our house. The city had good playing areas, green jungle, ever-flowing rivers, and hills as trekking destinations. We often used to go to the forest on nature trails and eat natural fruits along the way.

During the evening, we played many games including Cricket, Football, Gulli Danda, and Gulla Chor. The last one was distantly similar to Kabaddi, with two teams playing together. Members of one team would stand in a certain pattern with spacing between two consecutive players, while members of another team would run from one place to another, aiming to stay untouched by the opposing team members who would try their best to catch them. We did not even realize that these games provided us with extensive exercise, *khel khel mein.* Games like these did not require any props, and we used to play during power cuts as well.

Reflecting on those days, I gained a clear idea that later, while working in senior roles in West Bokaro, I was inspired to constantly try to upgrade the quality of living from my childhood days in Jamshedpur.

One such improvement we implemented in West Bokaro was the installation of air conditioners (ACs) in medical wards. During those days, there was no AC in any ward in the hospital. We installed ACs in the maternity ward, a facility that was not available even in Jamshedpur at that time. Once a senior Union leader, who was the President of Tata Workers' Union (TWU), visited West Bokaro and saw the ACs in the medical wards. He was amused and impressed; upon his return to Jamshedpur, he mentioned this to the MD of Tata Steel, suggesting the installation of ACs in the medical wards of Tata Main Hospital as well. During one of his subsequent visits, the MD of Tata Steel asked me how I managed to get the ACs installed and where the idea came from, especially when even TMH had not considered it.

I smiled. Memories of some of these facilities being added by Tata Steel management in and around the city as I was growing up came to mind.

Being from Jamshedpur always brought a sense of pride to its inhabitants. I realized this while studying in BIT Sindri. As an example, while the rest of the students there wore *lungis*, we wore *pajamas*. Students from other cities or villages always knew not to mess with the guys from Jamshedpur; we were considered the smarter lot.

The city had much more to offer beyond parks and gardens to keep its inhabitants entertained. Apart from sports, children of Jamshedpur had just a few other sources of entertainment, one of which was watching a movie in a theater.

While I often used to see some of our neighboring families walk to one of the movie theaters to watch a new release, my father did not have a good impression of movies. I don't think he was wrong in his thinking, as movies were the primary media during those years in the absence of social media, which tended to distract young minds – and potentially pollute them to some extent. As a result, I do not recall having seen many movies. We used to study, participate in sports, play various games, and occasionally go out for dinner at nearby restaurants in Jamshedpur. Occasionally, my father would allow me to watch a movie with a neighboring family. One such movie I remember watching was "Naya Daur" featuring Dilip Kumar. Movies were very affordable in those days; a regular ticket cost *char anna* and a VIP ticket cost *aath anna*. Today's generations wouldn't understand the value of these coins. As families went for movies, they were also enticed by hotels near the theaters. Some eateries, especially Punjabi restaurants, also offered alcohol along with food. Most of these eateries were located in the Sakchi area as the city was slowly but steadily expanding.

As a child, I remember seeing only Basant and Kareem Talkies in the initial few years. Gradually, more cinema theaters such as Jamshedpur Talkies, Nataraj Theater, and Anil Talkies came up in the city.

One of my cousins was very fond of movies. Often, I would hear about movies while talking to them or to neighboring friends. But thanks to my father's strict rules, my exposure to movies was almost negligible throughout my growing up years in Jamshedpur.

We had quite a few clubs in Jamshedpur. Occasionally, I would visit some of these clubs with my family. They were more 'controlled' and safer places to visit, where one had to adhere to a certain dress code and behavior. The first two clubs were Golmuri Club – established since 1928 – and Telco Club. Besides these, United Club (converted from an old training institute), Bengal Club in Sakchi, and the club in Kadma were prominent evening destinations. While the club in Kadma had a 'Bengali flavor' to it, Beldih had an 'English culture.' Likewise, each club had a distinct culture and identity.

One of the factors that caught my attention was that you had to follow a specific dress code while visiting these clubs. Even inside a club, different areas had different dress codes. If you wished to go to the billiards room, you couldn't wear shorts. Similarly, you couldn't enter the bar in shorts. Outside the bar, those were the days of Dhoti and *Kurta*. Movies were screened inside the clubs on weekends. The food offered was quite distinct; British continental dishes were available in the clubs and not elsewhere. The culture was modern as people used to play Tennis.

Dress code also played an important role outside the clubs. I remember people used to dress formally while going to the office. T-shirts were not acceptable office attire; some people even wore ties back then. Workers on the shop floor used to wear shirts and khaki pants.

When growing up, we could see the well-knit society—a great mix of cultures.

You might have started to guess by now if all was just perfect and fairytale in this growing city. That was not the case and I do recall moments of despair and disappointment when reflecting on my years in Jamshedpur. To top all such moments with darker shades of gray, I have vivid memories of witnessing a riot in the city.

This occurred just after the 1965 war with Pakistan. Jamshedpur, being the hub of economic and industrial prosperity in the Eastern part of India, became a target. Pakistani jets had been spotted flying close to

Kalaikunda air force station near Kharagpur in West Bengal. Government sources had advised Tata Steel management to keep the city in hiding, especially at night, as it was easy to locate a lit-up city area from the sky. Arrangements were made to prevent the spread of street lights, with cylindrical covers provided below each light fitting. Every citizen was advised to switch off lights or cover house windows with thick, dark curtains to contain light within the houses. Tata Steel management also decided to cover chimneys in the factories to stay safe during emergencies.

We often take a sigh of relief when something untoward does not happen, only to be completely surprised by something unexpected. This is exactly what happened in this case.

Though the city remained safe during the war, something changed about the 'soul' of the city. The same city, which had such a coherent and homogenous culture, started seeing rifts. During the 1965 war, a lot of genocide or ethnic cleansing took place in Pakistan, where many Hindus and Sikhs were massacred. In Jamshedpur, we had a refugee colony. Some of the refugees who had come from Pakistan a couple of decades ago were living there, mostly from the Sikh community.

After the 1965 war, a train full of new refugees from East Pakistan (later becoming Bangladesh after the 1971 war) arrived at Jamshedpur station. People from their community came to welcome them, and some from another community protested their welcome or entry into the city.

This led to the outbreak of the first riot in Jamshedpur. At least, I had not seen anything like this before. I was around 14 years old then.

All hell broke loose, and we started hearing the sounds of 'Allah-o-Akbar,' 'Jai Bajrang Bali,' and 'Jai Bole So Nihal' from the forest area between Baridih—where we were living in the newly built colony—and the TELCO area. People who had been living as neighbors for years started killing each other. People began looting each other's properties after killing them. Luckily, the situation was brought under control with the intervention of local police and Tata security personnel, but something about the city had changed and was to haunt people for a long time.

It was a pathetic experience.

I experienced another riot in 1984—though smaller in scale—while living in West Bokaro. A disturbance had broken out in Ramgarh Cantt—an army area between West Bokaro and Ranchi—following the assassination of Prime Minister Mrs Indira Gandhi. On that day, we had gone to Ranchi to purchase household goods and groceries. While returning, just before the entry to Ramgarh Cantt on the highway, we were stopped at Kantatoli Chowk and asked to turn back. This meant we had to take an alternative route from Ranchi to West

Bokaro. We attempted to return via Kanke Road on the outskirts of Ranchi but got lost. We were advised to take yet another route. We returned to Ranchi without a single penny in our pocket, unprepared for this situation. Fortunately, I remembered one of our colleagues from West Bokaro, Digambar Jha, who owned a house in Ranchi and was also there at that time. I called him and asked for some money, which he provided, and then we stayed in a hotel. The next day, we took a new route via Patratu Valley and encountered Sikh men running across the road. We were afraid they might attack us, but thankfully, they did not harm us, and we reached West Bokaro safely, albeit shaken.

Apart from these exceptions, life in Jharkhand, especially in Jamshedpur, has been enjoyable. Even today, I feel nostalgic when recalling the beautiful memories we built while growing up in the city of Jamshedpur, which was, is, and will remain the dream child of the vision of Mr. J N Tata.

"Tata has set a benchmark for conducting business with care for people. Rarely has any other organization set an example where care for people is a fundamental part of a business group's strategy, inspiring organizations locally and globally."

CHAPTER FIVE

West Bokaro Diary (Part 1) – Into the Wild

I was born in Jamshedpur and spent my early childhood here.

I remember this place as one of the finest towns to live in.

In the previous chapter, I wrote about my life in Jamshedpur—my school, friends, neighbors, playgrounds, nearby shops, cinemas, clubs, dams for family picnics, parks for walks, and the zoo where I first saw wild animals.

Jamshedpur was truly a once-in-a-lifetime experience. It became synonymous with almost a perfect childhood for me. I still have many friends there, and every time I return, it feels like coming back home. I can still smell the memories woven during my childhood and youth. In my heart, I often thank my father for giving us the beautiful life of Jamshedpur. Anyone from the Eastern part of India knows how beautiful a town Jamshedpur is.

I didn't know it then, but another town subsequently played an even bigger role in shaping my life and career. It's another town set up by the Tatas, but many people still do not know about this place. I have already mentioned the name in the headline.

If someone is asked to list towns in the state of Jharkhand, they will likely think of Jamshedpur, Bokaro, Ranchi, Dhanbad, Hazaribagh, and a few others, but hardly anyone would think of a place that even I did not know would become one of the most important places in my life.

It has been more than four decades, but I still remember the day I arrived at the nondescript railway station of Ramgarh. Today, the town has an army cantonment area, market, good roads, and schools, but at the time I am speaking about, Ramgarh did not have any of these. The town became quiet after five in the evening, and the silence would only be broken by the whistle of the locomotive engine pulling the train of bogeys twice daily. The small railway station only allowed a two-minute stop, which was more than enough time to disembark as hardly anyone boarded or left the train there.

Lessons in Wilderness

When leaving Jamshedpur, I assumed that since I was going to another Tata town, there would be some similarities between the two, and life would not be that tough. However, as soon as I came out of the railway station and saw a taxi sent to pick me up, I realized where I was heading...

That was the beginning of a new chapter in my life.

I got into the taxi, which started moving on the main road and soon left the road to take an unmetalled lane through the forest that was not worthy of being called a road.

That was 1975.

Coming from Jamshedpur, I was unprepared for a place that did not even have a proper road. Jamshedpur, on the other hand, had beautiful, metaled roads lined with trees. It had playgrounds with swings, slides, merry-go-rounds, seesaws, and other outdoor equipments. It boasted some of the best schools in the Eastern part of India and well-maintained gardens.

Now, I was in another Tata town, but it had none of these—at least not yet. It was dark by the time I reached the town, and I wondered whether I would be able to work in this place for long.

Gradually, I discovered that the worst part of my experience was over, and now the better part was about to come. Though it took me a while to feel settled in the new place, meeting people who were no different from those I had met in Jamshedpur brought relief. People and culture are the biggest assets of the Tatas, and it was the same in all their locations.

Meeting people was a sigh of relief for me. I still remember some of the early people I met, with whom I later built strong bonds. They guided me so that I could settle safely and happily in the new place.

Today, when I look back, I have a suggestion for people from the new generation: do not make career choices solely based on location. You might be drawn to a new place, but your job experience might not align well. Ultimately, our job satisfaction deeply impacts our overall happiness. Make career decisions considering challenging roles, the work culture of the new company, and future growth opportunities. Avoid rushing into decisions based solely on superficial appearances; *not everything that glitters is gold.* Take your time to understand the role and explore the new environment; you might pleasantly discover that this was the best decision you ever made. The key point here is never to judge solely on face value, as those judgments could be misleading. Things, people, experiences, and jobs might appear glossy on the surface, but deeper understanding might reveal unattractive realities. Career decisions are crucial and should not be rushed.

Let me provide some examples:

If you join a new company and find the location unattractive, don't form a quick negative impression. Try to understand the advantages that the place might offer.

If you are in a department and dislike your role, make a list of positives and negatives to gain a balanced perspective.

If you are considering ending a relationship, take your time to understand both sides carefully.

In life, not all dreams come true. Identify your key priorities and base your decisions on whether those priorities are met. If they aren't, reconsider your decision or think about changing your approach. Take responsibility for improving certain aspects rather than leaving a job or place on superficial grounds if your main priorities are fulfilled.

Over the decades, I not only grew professionally at West Bokaro but also contributed to making it a better place to live and work.

Not a Love at First Sight

Ghatotand... the name doesn't exactly sound sweet, does it? I mean, when you say "Shimla," "Delhi," "Manali," "Switzerland," or even "Kohima" or "Calcutta," those names do sound appealing, don't they?

But then Shakespeare, the famous English playwright, poet, and actor, wrote, "What's in a name?" He further wrote, "That which we call a rose; By any other name would smell as sweet."

And he wasn't wrong. It just took me some time to understand what the great litterateur meant—in my case, in the context of Ghatotand.

Growing up in the beautiful city of Jamshedpur, I never knew I would end up spending a major part of my life in this small town surrounded by open-cast collieries, situated atop a mined out underground coal mine.

Jamshedpur showed me how beautiful life could be: wide roads, lush green trees lining the streets, playgrounds, sports stadiums, shopping areas, family clubs, and beautiful weekend getaways to picnic destinations—the place had it all.

Then, I completed my engineering course in an almost equally green, though smaller, town called Sindri, home to one of the most reputable engineering colleges in the region. I spent five years here studying mechanical engineering. During holidays, I would return to Jamshedpur to be with my family.

From these two green locales, I transitioned to Ghatotand to begin my career. This area was all about mining and was quite small, nestled in hilly terrain far removed from regular cities. The wide, long roads, sports stadiums, playgrounds, movie theaters, shopping areas, and golf courses—all vanished. It seemed like a town unto itself, isolated from the rest of the world.

It took me some time to realize that I was now in a small place in the Hazaribagh district of Jharkhand, lacking all the familiar facilities I was accustomed to. This was to become my destiny if I did not take action.

I began applying to other companies. I first applied to Bharat Heavy Electricals Limited (BHEL) and passed the written examination, but it seems my lack of networking or references hindered me during the final interviews. I was so accustomed to the Tata group culture that I had never felt the need to reach out to people from other major groups in the country. My contacts were limited, and this seemed to impede my progress in the final interviews.

I tried applying to other companies as well, but in the meantime, something interesting began to happen.

I started to see a new meaning in what Shakespeare had said over 400 years ago, in an entirely different part of the world.

Every place has its unique culture and pros and cons. I had so far seen the less inspiring side of West Bokaro. Now, it was time to explore the positives. I discovered that the place had a very close-knit society; families frequently gathered for get-togethers and celebrations. I began to build personal relationships with people. The wives of senior staff members were genuinely caring, and I gradually started to feel like part of a larger family.

On the work front, I had another pleasant surprise.

Unlike many larger organizations, West Bokaro had a unique work culture. Here, there was ample opportunity to learn from our mistakes, with colleagues teaching and mentoring us through our work experiences. This was a significant advantage of the place—I felt respected and welcomed. I also realized that the workmen held us in high regard. They took pleasure in assisting us with errands, even when we declined. There was a nearby chowk where workmen often gathered in the evenings for casual conversation and downtime. I discovered that my colleagues were concerned about my image as an officer, and they volunteered to fetch items from the chowk area that I would have otherwise visited myself. This was a new experience for me. Feeling so loved and respected was a sensation I had not encountered anywhere else—not even in Jamshedpur.

"That which we call a rose; by any other name would smell as sweet."

The place truly was sweet, and the name didn't matter.

Looking back now, I realize that the place had an unspoken '360-degree support system' for people like me. My manager, peers, team members, workmen, and even the family members of neighbors and colleagues welcomed me and made me feel like one of them.

I understood why wise individuals advise against judging something based solely on its appearance. One should take the time to understand people and places. It's an impatient world where people rarely invest the effort to delve deeper and truly understand anything.

As I became more familiar with West Bokaro, my affection for the place grew gradually, though not dramatically. That's how life is—less about sudden changes and more about gradual realizations.

In the next few months, I stopped applying for other jobs. It was as if the place whispered in my ear, "You are needed here. Stay with me. The place will embrace you more with time." Soon, I fell in love with the true character of the place. It was akin to someone marrying an 'ordinary-looking' person and initially feeling disappointed. However, with time, the individual discovers the intrinsic qualities and gradually falls in love. I think this is the reality of our world—some people and places have hidden inner beauty that unfolds over time. That's why they say good things take time.

The place also provided me with several great mentors who left a lifelong impact on my thought process and life.

In the mining industry, there are three areas of expertise: mining technology, mechanical machines, and electrical systems. Gradually, I was exposed to each of these areas. It seemed like West Bokaro had made up its mind to support me in every possible way. The things you love also love you back.

During my initial settling period, I encountered people who provided comfort and made me feel welcomed. Mr. A N Mitra and Mr. R S S Murthy were two such individuals who treated me like family, even at work. I have fond memories of my interactions with them.

As I settled into the new place over the following weeks, I gained three seniors who became my mentors in the three key areas mentioned earlier.

Mr. R S S Murthy became my mentor in mining engineering. He was a stern administrator during the day and an easy-going soul in the evening.

Mr. A N Mitra was a strict mentor and teacher in mechanical engineering. He made it really tough for youngsters like me as he probably knew that otherwise we would not have made the best use of our initial period of working and learning. We were fresh from the Engineering college where we had been taught a lot of theories. Had we not put the theories into practice by doing the hard work, we would not have gained confidence as an engineer. Initial few years of working in an organization are always vital for any fresh graduate from the college and I was lucky to have Mr A N Mitra as my manager. He challenged us and scolded us but made us work in the field and on the shop floor. Most importantly, he made us look at our profession with pride and respect. Later on in my career, I became the head of maintenance for a wide range of mechanical equipments in many 'quarries' (open cast mines) involving tens of crores of budget and my confidence as an engineer grew up. Mr A N Mitra's initial guidance and mentoring went a long way in shaping my career as an engineer and also as myself a mentor for coming generations, I had also known by now as how to coach young engineers who were to work under me in times to come.

I would like to cite a few examples of my 'unofficial mentoring sessions' with Mr A N Mitra. Once, Mr Mitra took me to a captive power plant at West Bokaro. The boiler (an important part of the power plant used to convert water into steam) was undergoing a shutdown but still it was hot from inside. I was shaken when Mr Mitra asked me to join him inside the boiler chamber. Those who have been to a power plant, know that it's a huge chamber indeed and people can walk inside it when it's not in operation. The shutdown had just begun and the inside chamber had still not cooled down completely. I remember feeling the heat and sweating uncontrollably as I entered. My cheeks turned as red as imported apples but I did not say a thing and listened to Mr Mitra who explained the concept of a coal-fired boiler so clearly. The entire concept of steam and electricity generation became clear to me during that half an hour. That is the kind of tough love which is required to really soil our hands and learn the 'tricks of the trade' in any field of life and career.

It was obvious that Mr Mitra used to lead by example as he himself came inside the boiler along with me for giving me a demonstration of how a steam power plant works.

Let me cite another example. I remember, once there was a shutdown of ropeway. There were two types of ropeways in West Bokaro – Monocable and Tri cable, which were used as cost effective, time efficient and environment friendly mode for the transportation of coal. The shutdown or breakdown maintenance of the ropeways used to prolong for many days and people had to work on almost 24x7 basis. During one of such shutdowns, Mr Mitra was supervising the work and he stayed there on the site for three consecutive days. Finally, he got so tired that while standing on a heap of coal on the third day, he dozed off. No body including him realized this till there was a sound of someone falling. People looked around and found Mr Mitra getting up on all fours from the heap. He had slept while standing and had fallen on the mound of coal.

That was the kind of work ethic I saw in my mentors.

Today, when I see people watching so many inspirational videos and reading self-help books to know the secrets of success and to keep themselves motivated, I smile. The secrets of success are just a few and one of them is surely the bone-cracking hard work while staying put in the work field till you think you just can't continue any further, just like Mr Mitra did. One secret of success is surely going beyond your comfort zone and not only doing things which are easy. You succeed when you persist while others have given up. It's about learning through all your life and upgrading your work. It's about developing a strong mindset which never gives up even if the difficulties surround you from all sides. If you don't have a strong mindset, be ready to live a mediocre life.

The secrets are just a few including 'doing it by hand' and learning by actually seeing and feeling it – just like I experienced along with Mr Mitra when we spent some time inside the boiler chamber. Success is nothing but sheer hard work and going the distance where others give up. It's about knowing our work and mastering our skills well. People around us will make fun of us if they see our weakness.

You need to be mentally and physically strong. The world never supports the weak. Even Gods will not support the weak as is evident from the following shloka:

अश्वं नैव गजं नैव व्याघ्रं नैव च नैव च
अजापुत्रं बलिं दधातु देवो दुर्बलाघतक:

Ashwam naiva, Gajam naiva, Vyagram naiva cha naiva cha
Ajaputram balim dadhatu devo durbala ghatakaha

Not horse, not elephant, not tiger, but only the goat is sacrificed in a ritual.

God also does not protect the weak.

If you are weak like a goat, be ready to be sacrificed. Hence, the only way forward in life is to transform yourself to a stronger version of yourself.

And how to stay strong like an elephant or tiger, as mentioned in the shloka above? It's simple – keep learning, keep working hard, keep building a strong network, keep delivering results and let people know about this in a subtle yet clear way. Keep setting goals and planning for it. Be disciplined and do what you say. Keep building skills which make you rare and high in demand.

Now tell me – do you really need to watch so many motivational videos? The secrets of success are all around us. It's just that only a few, like Mr Mitra did, 'can stay strong and stay put for many days without taking a break.'

Another mentor who shaped my life by influencing me positively was Mr V K Sharma, also known as 'Vicky,' among peers and friends.

Vicky was a dynamic, energetic, and confident leader who was very popular among the people of West Bokaro. Unlike Mr A N Mitra, he was extremely warm and energetic in his approach. Nowadays, people speak a lot about empowerment. Mr Sharma empowered me abundantly. I had full freedom to make decisions and manage the work I wanted to do. This was another kind of mentoring where morally, I felt responsible to be right every single time, as someone trusted me and supported my decisions wholeheartedly. He used to pitch in whenever I needed guidance, and otherwise, he never intervened. At times, when I made a mistake, he used strong words, but on the same day, he also invited me for a drink at the officers' club. He was not a micromanager. As I did more work, I learned more along the way. This was another way of mentoring – and it was a very effective way to let people grow – which I experienced while working under Mr V K 'Vicky' Sharma.

As I mentioned above, Mr Sharma often invited me for a drink at the officers' club in the evening. He was a master conversationalist and used to engage us in talks on various topics from around the world. These evenings were a great stress reliever after a long day dealing with the same and often repeated work matters in the office. We rejuvenated while laughing, chatting, and sipping our drinks endlessly.

Yes, the club in West Bokaro was another big draw for us. Great food, great drinks, and great friends to hang out with. Often, women also used to join us there, and we had some lovely times as one family of West Bokaro.

Today, when I look back and think about the two distinct styles of mentoring, I feel grateful to Mr Mitra and Mr Sharma for making me a better professional and also a fulfilled human being who enjoyed his work and life.

Another mentor I would like to speak about is Mr R L Singhal, who was an electrical engineering veteran and taught me the basics of electrical systems. This proved handy as I later took up the responsibility of end-to-end maintenance of machines in the colliery, where electricals were a significant part of the maintenance work.

The journey of my mentoring does not stop here. I also had a few 'mentors' who taught me some valuable lessons despite not intending to do so. With a good learning mindset, you can learn from good mentors and from people who may not be so inspiring. Just as we learn a lot from failures and challenges, we also learn a lot from people who may not like us. But with a positive mindset of learning from them – often in the form of learning what one should not do – we can also bring these people on our side.

But more about this in the next chapter.

"We all meet various people in our lives. With a mindset of learning from people, we can get better. Unfortunately, most people, due to their own ego, cease to learn from others and grow. Let's identify our mentors and stay in touch with them, as they add a lot of value to our lives."

CHAPTER SIX

West Bokaro Diary (Part 2) – Out of India

Technology, Culture, and Change

Recently, one of my ex-colleagues sent me a link to a news clipping on WhatsApp. It was wrapped in nostalgia and read like this: "Further to its statement in March 2020 that it was considering the closure of the historic Luenen underground coal mining equipment factory, the associated Wuppertal operations, as well as the former O&K factory in Dortmund which produces hydraulic mining shovels, Caterpillar confirmed in August 2020 that the plants will be shuttered."

Dortmund and O&K!

These two words caught my attention. Dortmund is a beautiful place in Germany, and O&K was a German company—or perhaps, it was a German company, as it would have been closed by now.

This news brought back old memories and reminded me of how change impacts companies and people. It also took me down memory lane to when I had visited the O&K factory in Dortmund, along with one of my colleagues, Naresh Prasad, in the early 1990s. This visit was part of my work in the field of equipment maintenance, where I was entrusted with the responsibility of technological upgrading of shovels or excavators, which are crucial equipment in a mining division.

But how did we end up in Germany from the wilderness of West Bokaro? Let me start from the beginning.

'Shovels' or 'Excavators' are common words for anyone working in a mining area. These are almost buzzwords for any mining engineer. These heavy machines are used to dig out large chunks of overburden (the top layers of soil consisting of rocks and debris) or coal and load them onto rear dumpers or coal haulers for transportation out of the collieries to dumping plants.

Shovels are also one of the most visible examples of technological advancements, as they are unique and giant-like in size compared to regular mobile machines like cars that you normally see in your vicinity.

When I joined West Bokaro, these machines were heavily used, albeit of slightly older technology. The machines we had at West Bokaro were sourced from Heavy Industry Corporation (HEC), Ranchi, which had adopted the technology of 'rope-operated shovels' from Russian technical experts. These were electric rope shovels, which were bulkier with lower availability, productivity, and higher maintenance costs. In comparison—as we later learned—hydraulic shovels were in demand, and both Germany and Japan were leading in the technological advancement of shovels. These countries had pioneered the design and manufacturing of state-of-the-art hydraulically operated shovels, and it was essential for us to upgrade our machines with the changing technology. After conducting due diligence, a proposal was made to study and import hydraulic shovels from O&K, Germany.

Dortmund is a small and beautiful place in Germany, famous for the O&K factory. I visited the place to understand the technology of shovels and present the proposal to replace our existing old shovels back home upon my return. This visit was a challenging task, and I was both excited at the thought of visiting a new foreign city and tense at the prospect of absorbing as much as I could to ensure the success of the technological upgrade project.

Before traveling, I conducted some research about Dortmund and O&K. The internet was almost non-existent in those days, so I had to rely on colleagues who had visited and some magazines. Most of the knowledge I gained about the place and the company came much later after I visited and spent a few days there.

Dortmund had quite a history behind it. The city was founded in 882 AD and had become one of Germany's most important centers for coal, steel, and beer production; consequently, it was one of the most heavily bombed cities in Germany during World War II. Often, resourcefulness and prosperity become your undoing as you come into the limelight and attract unwanted attention. While we speak of a city, this is also true for many people—it's a connected world, after all. The rich and powerful are often targeted the most by various power centers and are frequently in the eye of the storm and media glare. Some people take this concept to a personal level by not showing off their wealth or fortune, lest it invite bad omens.

Obviously, Dortmund had many stories hidden within it. It is said that the devastating bombing raids of 12 March 1945, which included 1,110 aircraft of Allied forces, destroyed 98% of buildings in the city center.

These raids were the largest for a single target in the entire World War II.

Like Dortmund, even O&K had a history behind it.

Orenstein & Koppel (usually abbreviated to O&K) was a major German engineering company specializing in railway vehicles, escalators, and heavy equipment. It was founded on April 1, 1876, in Germany—long before the world had witnessed any of the World Wars—by two gentlemen, Mr Benno Orenstein and Arthur Koppel. Thanks to the entrepreneurial spirit of these two enthusiastic and technically capable individuals, the company soon became known around the world for its high-end, technologically advanced hydraulic shovels, which were renowned for requiring less maintenance and being ruggedly durable with higher productivity.

I still remember my first experience when I reached Germany. The breeze in Dusseldorf was crisp and cool as we disembarked from the aircraft. That was my first experience of traveling to Europe. I was with my colleague, who was also unfamiliar with European countries. As we exited the airport, we were struck by the stark difference between West Bokaro, the place we came from, and Dusseldorf, the place we had landed in—the latter was known for its rich culture, keen sense of fashion, and its prominence as a commercial hub. Its annual trade shows and exhibitions were world-famous. The place looked so neat and clean that we could hardly think of any place in India that could match its neatness.

We soon learned that the place was also known for its fast driving. Or rather, speed was an 'in-thing' throughout Germany—or to be more precise, throughout Europe. After all, you find some of the best quality roads and technologically advanced cars there!

No sooner had we come out of the airport than we found a car waiting for us, sent by our host (O&K), and one of its officials welcomed us warmly—a gesture we didn't expect to encounter in Germany. We had been told that Germany is a place where people smile less and keep their work and personal lives separate. They believe in finishing their tasks on time, and unlike in India, overtime is rare there. This means you'll hardly see people sharing jokes, gossiping, or smiling excessively at work. Therefore, our host's warm smile made us feel a bit more comfortable, as for us Indians, smiles, laughter, and conversation are a part of daily life.

We got into the car, which quickly sped onto the highway leading toward the city where O&K's office and factory were located. The road was smooth, and the traffic was less intense and more disciplined than anything we had ever seen in India. For this reason, it was quite common for most drivers to exceed speeds of 130 kilometers per hour. Germany is also the birthplace or innovation lab for some of the best and most luxurious car brands. The car we were in was so good and smooth that if we hadn't been looking out through the windows, it would have been difficult to imagine that we were cruising at such a speed—I could never have imagined this in India. I'm talking about a high speed where one can drive and still feel safe on the road.

This is one reason why I always feel that traveling to foreign countries is a great opportunity to explore parts of the world that we would never know exist unless we visit these countries. The discipline of driving, quality of roads, appearance of cars, technological advancements, the beauty of the surroundings, and natural getaways are always an eye-opening experience. Seeing these in pictures is one thing, but living through those experiences is an entirely new and exhilarating feeling.

Little did I know then that later in my career with Tata Steel, I would visit many countries both in the East and West and see a new world, having enriching and novel experiences. But about those, I will share later in this book.

Our beautiful car trip came to an end rather too soon. It didn't take more than an hour from Dusseldorf to Dortmund.

We were directed to a guest house where we were with people from different countries, especially from Germany and Korea. Language was a significant barrier as we heard English, German, and Korean being spoken all at the same time in the dining hall. Our English was often of no use there. *When the going gets tough, the tough get going.* Nobody knows who said this American proverb first—John F. Kennedy's father or the American football coach K. Rockne! But it was surely action time for us, and we had to implement this in life then and there.

However, we also discovered that there are certain words—and actually just a few—that made complete and clear sense when spoken by people from any nationality. The word 'Beer' was understood by anyone and everyone there. We later understood why! Germany is the home of beer, and Germans are very particular about their finely crafted brews. The German Purity Law ensures clearly regulated ingredients for beer. Anything else is not beer—simple as that! The ingredients are water, malt, hops, and yeast. This is known as the pure promise of quality in Germany.

Aside from the rare examples of 'beer' that made communication easy, we had to be tough and innovative to make the most of our time with the German strangers.

We found many creative ways to keep things going, whether in technical discussions or in the dining halls. As often happens in the face of challenges, we became extraordinarily creative in finding ways to make things happen and keep communication flowing smoothly. I even surprised myself with my drawing abilities when I sketched a chicken in a bowl of curry on a piece of paper to show the chef and ask for some extra curry. And this was just the beginning of my sketching saga. However, we were not the only ones struggling. I noticed Koreans also carrying a 'Korean to English' dictionary to order what they wanted. It was a funny situation, with Koreans not knowing English and us, of course, not knowing Korean, all while being in a country where German was the primary language. But soon, the all-women staff in the restaurants became fans of our sketches, and it gradually became easier for us to convey what we wanted to say. What was initially a challenge turned into fun with sketches and drawings.

Over the next few days, the idea of 'sketch and show' actually worked, as pictures, like music, have no language! Keeping a pen and paper handy became a habit for us. I wasn't very skilled at making sketches, but as Benjamin Franklin said, "Necessity is the mother of invention." Soon, I began to enjoy making sketches.

During our technical discussions, we were thoroughly impressed with German designs. In general, through our interactions—which were later validated by actual operations in West Bokaro—we found that O&K designs were strong and efficient. There was no chance of structural failure, and the number of hoses was kept to a minimum to reduce downtime as much as possible. It was expected to give us higher availability and productivity.

Every meeting with new people and visit to never-seen-before places teaches us new lessons. Our visit to Germany taught us many. Let me share a few:

Going to a new place or meeting a new person is always a novel experience and brings discomfort and a certain degree of anxiety to your mind. You do not know how the lead person from the visiting company or the lead is going to treat you. You are wondering what you should say and how you should behave not to look out of place or face a 'not so funny' situation. I see a connection here. People say that nothing grows within the comfort zone. When we visit a new place, do a new task, or meet a new person, we face the same anxiety. That means – you are no longer working within your comfort zone. This is one of the common secrets of growth and success in life. It always begins with butterflies in the stomach. Hence, every time you feel nervous, be sure something new is happening. Be excited and look at it positively. Put in extra effort, do some preparation, and face the situation with a smile as these are at the core of transformation in life and career. Rather, you should ask yourself – when was the last time I did something for the first time? And you should be doing something new, talking to a new person, reading a new book, visiting a new place, and undergoing a new experience as frequently as feasible. This is surely a great way of living a complete life with all its colors.

German people work in factories to complete the task at hand within a stipulated time period. They do not care for working overtime and do not delay jobs in regular shifts to get some extra overtime. They are punctual and disciplined. Maybe the reason is – being a developed nation, their per capita income is more, and hence their focus is on time and work-life balance. In India, due to low income and no social and financial security system, people do all that is feasible to make some extra bucks. This often leads to people being 'over-willing' to work extra and make some extra money. Work-life balance and often physical and emotional health take the back seat. We have every right to say that our country is great. We have every right to say – *"mera Bharat mahaan."*

However, we should also be willing to accept that there are many things which we can learn from other countries. Just like we can learn new things from other people, we can and must be willing to learn new lessons from new places. I became a lifelong fan of discipline, process-centricity, and focus at work after my visit to Germany. Not that I did not follow these earlier as well, but I saw these qualities being on display without any exception in all circumstances by all the people that I met. And I saw the outcomes of these qualities on the shop floor. This gave me a lifelong reminder of how powerful these traits are. For me, being in maintenance, these became principles for life. Maintenance is all about a disciplined, process-centric, and focused approach, and the results are in black and white. A breakdown of a machine, which may cost hard cash due to less production, will stare you in the face if you don't follow some of these tenets like the commandments of professional work.

Germans do not like to mix fun with business. You won't hear laughter or jokes during work discussions. In India, such things are common over a cup of tea to break the monotony. We mix work and life and dilute both. If you join any Stress Management Seminar in India, chances are high that people will talk about how they get calls from their boss at six in the morning or ten at night, and frequently on weekends. If you've worked in the corporate world, you know how people spend a long time chit-chatting over a cup of tea or mug of coffee during office hours. You know how people just hang around at workstations of various people and promote this behavior. People feel guilty while applying for leave, and bosses do not mind canceling leaves at the last minute. In Germany, people value their private life, and intrusion into personal lives is not welcome.

Germans' discipline in social life is incredible. During my stay, I did not hear even one car honking on the road. They follow road discipline but will not honk unnecessarily. They will stop the car to give preference to pedestrians. Once, I saw an old lady crossing the street. All the cars stopped a few meters before the crossing point and waited patiently until the lady crossed the road. In India, recently I was crossing the road. I could see a flurry of vehicles honking and rushing toward me even as the traffic signal was yellow.

The Beginning of Technological Exploration

I don't know how many people actually appreciate it, but life is all a network of interconnected dots. A happening today is an outcome of something that happened a long time ago, and what we are doing today is going to lead to events that may unfold many years ahead in the future. By the time we see those events unfolding, the people who actually 'sowed the seeds' of those events would have moved to other places, and hence people cannot connect the dots, and to the 'normal eyes' or to the world at large, these events appear to be 'one-off events' which happen out of pure luck or just pop up out of nothing.

Hence, what the world sees as a standalone and disconnected set of events is actually interconnected if we pay attention and look at the history and present of human evolution.

We can cite multiple examples – what the British did many years ago to our education system has a long-lasting impact that we can experience even now. Many freedom fighters sacrificed their lives and happiness, and today we reap the benefits. In this book, I have spoken about how one act of courage of my father to get educated and move out of the village opened a new path for me as well as for my children and also for forthcoming generations.

It's indeed an interconnected world, and our global meetings and visits with technical experts related to the field of the mining industry and machinery which started in the early 1980s also had an interesting connection with the past. Let me elaborate on this a bit.

West Bokaro division was first started in the year 1946. As per the initial mining plans prepared for the site, it was to be first developed as an underground mine. The plan was to first mine out the lower seams of coals followed by doing open-cast mine in later decades. For the uninitiated, any coal mining belt or area normally has multiple horizontal layers of coals, the layers being known as coal seams. Each coal seam is situated below the earth's top surface at a certain depth, adjacent seams being separated by a few meters of rock and debris known in mining terminology as overburden. Coal seams originate and are formed by the consolidation of biota (the animal and plant life of a particular region), minerals, and natural chemicals through geologic time. Various forces of nature like compression, heat, sedimentation, erosion, and chemical energy result in the formation of coal. Multiple coal seams can exist in a reserve, with each coal seam separated by sedimentary rock or the noncoal layers which are usually sandstone, limestone, shale, siltstone, and mudstone.

By the time I joined the place, underground mining had given way to the open cast mining method which was found to be an economical way of mining coal as the top coal seams were at a shallow depth in and around West Bokaro. Also, open-cast mining method was more efficient as unlike in case of underground mining method in which only 66% of coal could be excavated, in open-cast mining, 100% of coal could be taken out. This was simply because in underground mining, coal pillars had to be left intermittently to prevent the roof from caving in.

These reasons, coupled with a few more, led to the application of heavy earth moving machines (HEMM) in mining areas.

But there was a problem – the heavy earth moving machines were now operating on top seams below which lower seams had already been mined out using the underground mining method in almost all areas. As a result, there was always a danger of machines caving in and falling in the tunnels created due to the excavation of coals. The machines were actually moving on a few feet of overburden layers above the empty tunnels caused by the mined out coal seams.

The topmost seam of coal in West Bokaro was seam no ten at most of the places. At a few locations, we also had 12th and 13th seams available for mining. Below 10th seam, there was an overburden layer of 9-10 meters which was to support the movement of shovels. At certain places where the thickness of overburden was lower, there were instances of machines caving in and tilting thereby suffering severe damage to the boom lift and other hydraulic components. Not only that, once the machine caved in and tilted, we had to use a dozer to pull the shovels using steel ropes tied to the main frame of the shovel. This often resulted in serious structural damage to the shovels. Since most of the areas where we had open-cast mines were above the underground mining zones, this was a pretty rampant problem.

Hence, the lower the pressure a machine exerted on the ground, the better and safer it was. The existing old types of electric rope shovels used to exert a pressure of 200 tons on the ground. We had heard that hydraulic O&K

shovels, if purchased, would only exert slightly above 100 tons of pressure. This would drastically enhance the safety of our mining operations. We could further reduce the pressure by choosing shovels with a smaller bucket capacity. Shovels with a higher bucket capacity, around 6-6.5 cubic meters, applied a pressure of 100 tons, which could be reduced to 80 tons if we opted for smaller shovels with a four cubic meters bucket capacity.

Another benefit of exploring hydraulic shovels was increased machine productivity due to less downtime, resulting in fewer planned and unplanned maintenance hours.

The combination of 'Higher Productivity' and 'Lower Pressure' provided an irresistible incentive that we simply could not ignore. This drove our visits to some of the most advanced manufacturing sites for designing and constructing heavy earth moving machines.

Hence, the transition from underground to open-cast mining processes was one of the key reasons we reached out to and visited global factories manufacturing shovels and other excavation and material handling machines. While we had visited some mines in India, we did not encounter such groundbreaking mining practices. Tatas are always known for being leaders in adopting new machines and practices, which was another reason we decided to procure machines that were second to none.

In a nutshell, the history of underground mining at this site led to a complete technological transformation of HEMMs during our time.

Making Effective Presentations

Apart from introducing state-of-the-art technology in shovels – and, of course, in other mining equipment – I also worked closely with teams to upgrade other machines in the coal processing and handling value chain. This included replacing truck transportation – which heavily polluted the environment – with conveyor belts and ropeways. I recall one such incident full of interesting experiences and lessons that I would like to share here.

While establishing the coal transportation system in West Bokaro, we proposed a certain budget for management consideration and approval. However, management only agreed to fund 85% of the amount, which was a substantial sum at that time. The 15% budget shortfall forced us to opt for ropeways instead of more advanced conveyors. Those familiar with ropeways understand how challenging and time-consuming their maintenance can be. A routine shutdown would require tens or hundreds of people working day and night for many days or weeks. A breakdown would put significant pressure on the entire system and would require at least a couple of weeks to rectify, with people working tirelessly on-site without breaks for days.

I often wonder that had we received that additional amount (a few crores of rupees), we would have replaced one of the ropeways with a conveyor belt and another with a railway line. We had two ropeways, and both were a constant threat to production and dispatches. Both were cost-efficient means of material handling compared to transportation by trucks. They also caused the least damage to the environment by keeping the generation of dust to a minimum. However, any breakdown in the ropeways used to disrupt the entire system, extending up to Jamshedpur, as the time and resources needed to restore the system were significant.

When we were seeking a budget to replace the ropeways with conveyors and a railway line, we somehow could not convince the management because those additional crores were a substantial amount in those days. With more foresight, we could have justified these expenses to have a more streamlined system in place. However, despite trying several times, we could not secure those additional sanctions and had to stick with ropeways.

I realized something during those days – if you are making a presentation to request more money and your business unit does not play a crucial role in the overall growth of the organization, your plea will not be taken seriously. At the time of our proposal, West Bokaro was an 'average' contributor to Tata Steel. It did not have the kind of 'aura' which it gained in later years. I will discuss this 'aura' more in the coming chapters.

This also reminds me of another chapter of 'failed sanction requests.' I remember one of the former heads of West Bokaro was seeking an investment of a certain amount for the opening of a new quarry block in West Bokaro. The then Managing Director of Tata Steel Limited, who was chairing a workshop in Goa and had invited senior leaders with their wives, did not even listen to the complete presentation. He said, "I am not going to listen to the whole presentation. I am going out to watch the sunset." Some of us felt sorry for the leader of West Bokaro who made the presentation. His request was valid, but perhaps the case was not presented adequately at an inappropriate time. We were asking for an amount equivalent to the company's profit at the time, half of which came from the sale of secondary products! If we had presented the case by demonstrating how this block would replace much costlier imported coal, thereby providing a cost advantage, and proposed a phased investment approach to offset the initial seemingly high investment, the outcome of the presentation might have been different and much better. Also, the timing of the presentation matters. You cannot capture the audience's attention when the sun is setting over the sea in beautiful Goa 😊. Perhaps one could have requested a different time slot, maybe in the morning the next day. You might think it's a light-hearted comment, but it also has a serious connection with how human psychology works.

This brings us to a few points to keep in mind before making a proposal or presentation to an authority. I am sharing these in case young and budding leaders can glean some insights from them.

For the successful presentation of any initiative or project in your hands, you need to consider the following:

- Have you conducted thorough work with data and evidence? Senior leaders will look for data and evidence rather than your opinion. You need to have done thorough and diligent work so that you can back up your claims with strong data.
- Have you demonstrated sufficient benefits or return on investment for the budget you are seeking? Be innovative and try to make it as lucrative and feasible as possible by phasing out the investments over a longer time frame. This will allow you to show the initial benefits of the investments to the deciding panel, instilling additional confidence in the leadership team and making it easier for them to consider your proposal.
- Before making the presentation, ask yourself whether you are fully convinced of the idea. If you yourself are not fully 'sold' on the idea, you will not be able to sell it to others. Your conviction in your idea, which of course will come after due diligence and hard work on the project, is a must for convincing others.

– Do you have a strong track record of past accomplishments? Are you someone who follows through on commitments? If you have a track record of delivering on promises, there is a higher likelihood that the board will take your demands more seriously. Your work should speak for itself, reflecting strong credentials derived from outstanding performance. This earns you credibility and makes people more inclined to listen to you.

– Are you certain it's the right time to make the presentation? 'Striking while the iron is hot' is crucial. The timing of the presentation matters significantly. If the company is facing financial difficulties and you are considering a presentation to ask for more funding, it may be wise to postpone your presentation until you believe it's the right time to 'sell' your idea. Alternatively, if you feel that for some reason, the company is focusing on a priority closely related to your idea, then the time for your idea has also come! Be astute and confident about these aspects. It helps.

CHAPTER SEVEN

West Bokaro Diary (Part 3) – Cycles of Life

Everything we attain in life is through a cycle of pain and realizations. Nothing ever grows within the comfort zone. I knew this, like many people do, but I didn't fully realize its power in my personal life until the storm of changes hit me, my friends, and colleagues in the early 2000s. Change is the only constant – many people talk about it, but I doubt if, except for a few, others truly grasp the power behind this word.

You can experience change positively or negatively. You can either run away from waves out of fear or run toward them with a surfing board in your hand.

When the wind of change blows, you can either build a wall and hide behind it, or you can build windmills and harness the power of this wind to make the world better.

When you face something challenging in your life, you can either run away from it or stay brave in the face of it. If you choose the former, you fade into oblivion. If you choose the latter, you become stronger and wiser. Champions certainly choose the latter, and that is what defines why they are champions!

Another thing that many can't fathom is that change is the only factor behind the growth of this world. Anything significant happening anywhere is because of change.

Now, that's interesting. Think of someone who has failed an examination. They can either go into a closed room and cry until they lose themselves, or they can do the following…

They go to a garden, spread their arms, and look up. Then they take a deep breath and thank God for the many blessings already in their life: a family to support them, parents to sponsor further studies, a healthy body and mind to keep them going, talents in areas where they excel, and the fact that they have a home whereas many don't. They remember the last time they received acclaim for something they did. They think of more blessings because everyone in this world, without exception, has many blessings they may have forgotten to count due to the clouds of doubt that surround us all.

Then they decide to make changes in their life going forward. They decide to adjust their habits and start waking up earlier in the morning to study. This means they will sleep earlier at night, avoiding wasting time on social media, streaming platforms, and unnecessary negative TV channels. They decide to seek guidance from a senior student as a coach. If needed, they decide to ask their father for tuition in one of the tougher subjects. They choose to eat healthily to boost their energy. They are all set to transform their life and career.

You can well imagine that now the student, not despite but because of the failed examination, is going to become a better student and perform much better in forthcoming examinations.

That's how people become better and more successful after facing challenges in life and career. All it requires is a winning mindset. Having the right coach is another powerful way to seek greatness in life.

I was working in West Bokaro as the head of one of the quarries. For those unfamiliar, a quarry is an open-cast mine. You might have seen some action sequences shot in an open-cast pit in movies like KGF, Dasara, Gunday, Drishyam, etc. The quarries are filled with heavy earthmoving machines, dust, and continuous digging action happening day and night. The location where I was working was responsible for supplying coal to the steel plant in Jamshedpur.

West Bokaro is a beautiful place, and I will be writing more about it in other chapters. Here, I want to speak about the sudden change in atmosphere toward the beginning of the millennium. It was a place where people used to be busy in their offices and quarries throughout the day, congregating in the club for a leisurely evening. Spending time in the bar, chatting about work and life, was a favorite pastime. Life was peaceful when the rumor mills slowly started working.

The world was celebrating the conquering of the Y2K problem when the work-and-peace-loving people of West Bokaro started seeing the emergence of a new challenge.

People began speaking about a new initiative launched across the place, known as PEP or 'Performance Ethics Program.' Evening talks revolved around the theme of this being just a fancy and casual name given to an otherwise career-threatening organization-wide assessment center program. Despite the core committee trying to communicate that it was just another program to 'create a strategic turnaround for the future growth of the organization,' rumor mongers were busy spreading news that it was related to 'sacking of old-timers and elevating youngsters.' They discussed the possibility of seniors being made to report to juniors after the PEP and some of the oldies being asked to leave as well. It was a way of gossiping but, as you know, there is no smoke without fire.

For a company like Tatas, it was shocking news. People had always believed that there would never be a time when individuals would be asked to leave the company. They always believed that people would never be treated in a manner they would be uncomfortable with under the new structure.

But now, change—a real big-time change—was in the air.

Today, when I look back and think of PEP, which was actually an assessment Center, I can connect my subsequent success to those challenging days.

People had read about these changes, but now they were about to undergo a personal experience of how threatening and discomforting changes could be.

I remember, after initial discomfort, I started preparing myself for the upcoming assessment Center. I reflected a lot on my strengths and the possibilities in front of me. Self-awareness was important because I knew I didn't have to pretend to be someone else in an assessment Center; that would make things worse. I had to be myself and had to do so confidently and 'enjoyably.' Yes, enjoyably, because once you look at challenges as opportunities, you can enjoy the experience by flowing with the flow and not thinking too much about adverse consequences. Once you know yourself well, decide to play on your strengths rather than focusing on weaknesses, and also decide to learn and grow as a person and professional with a deep sense of humility, you slowly become free from the unnecessary worries of life and career.

A positive mindset can make all the difference, and this is exactly how things unfolded for me.

I was ranked highly during the assessment Center, and this experience became the stepping stone for me to later become the General Manager of the Division.

Initial sense of uncertainty and doubt had given way to the days for which I can only be grateful today. Had the PEP not happened, I probably would not have grown in my career to the extent I did. The experience brought me in the view of top leadership team and I was given some challenging and senior level assignments and positions.

Challenges can be seen as opportunities for growth and development. They give us a chance to learn from what is happening and respond in a positive way. Taking on new challenges can be frightening, but it is important to test our limits and capabilities. However, people often focus on the fear and probable harm from challenges and not on the possibilities and positives of challenges.

In other words, challenges can help us grow and develop as individuals by pushing us out of our comfort zones and forcing us to learn new skills. They can also help us build resilience and develop a more positive outlook on life

Today, on reflection, I would like to make the following suggestions to people to turn their challenges into opportunities:

Create a plan: When you sit down and think about a plan of action, you think ahead to the possible solutions.

Your focus shifts from problems and fears to solutions and opportunities. If you were to imagine your future, the person and life you desire to have, what steps do you need to take to get there? Make a plan to overcome challenges. There is no point in sitting and freezing in anticipation of fear and danger.

Increase awareness: Be aware of your thoughts and feelings. This will help you identify when you are getting overwhelmed or stressed. In this case, I got as much information as feasible about the upcoming assessment center and what kind of environment they created. It made me relatively more comfortable as I could get rid of major part of uncertainties.

Appreciate and be grateful: Accept where you are now and what you have. This is your life, at this time. While it's temporary, it's still your life. Appreciate what you have and be grateful for it. Also, accept the actions which you can take and be grateful for the very fact that you are getting the opportunities to appear for the assessment center. You are getting these opportunities because you are working in a great organization and that itself is a reason to celebrate. There are many who will never make it to the level of life which you are blessed with. Having an attitude of gratitude in itself is good enough a reason for you to feel better.

Create momentum, gradually: Take small steps toward your goal every day. This will help you build momentum and keep moving forward. There is no need for you to take massive actions in the beginning. Take small steps and keep doing so. Taking incremental steps on a consistent basis is the best way to gain momentum, steadily but surely.

Take lots of action: The more action you take, the more progress you will make toward your goal. The more progress you make, the less afraid you are. The less afraid you are, the more emotionally in control you feel, and the more confident you become. This, in turn, leads to success. Being in a state of action or doing things is the best way to reduce fear and enhance your chance of success. In other words, taking action is the most important lever for you to convert your challenges into opportunities.

Ask others: Don't be afraid to ask for help when you need it. Whether it's from a friend, family member, or professional, asking for help can make all the difference in overcoming challenges. I have always believed in mentoring others and also seeking mentorship from people senior to me. Never refrain from seeking help and support.

Stay positive: Always maintain a state of gratitude and positivity as you work toward your goals. Keep positive thoughts about the challenges you face. Instead of dwelling on negative outcomes, focus on positive solutions. You will find that these positive thoughts keep you smiling, positive, and strong. I observed many people who were fearful of the PEP, not gaining anything from it.

Conversely, I saw many others who looked upon it with excitement, turning it into one of the biggest milestones of their career.

Now, I have a question for you.

Can you think of a PEP-like situation in your life?

A situation that made you afraid of the consequences?

Can you think of 3-5 such situations that challenged you?

It could be an examination, a mountaineering expedition, a new career opportunity, a sports event, a new venture, or a new company that you considered starting.

Consider your feelings before starting your journey.

Consider the factors that contributed to your success in these situations.

Consider the factors that led to losses in some of these situations.

What were the factors that contributed to winning or losing?

Reflect on these and try to connect the points I have mentioned in this chapter.

"Reflection is key, and I encourage you to reflect extensively on how to turn your challenges into opportunities. If you grasp this point, you will be a winner throughout your life.

This chapter is not about the Performance Ethics Program or PEP; it's about developing a 'Winning Mindset' – a mindset that will enable you to view every challenge as a stepping stone to climb higher by seeing the opportunities ahead."

CHAPTER EIGHT

West Bokaro (Part 4) – Lessons in Remoteness

I have spent a major part of my career working in the Raw Material Divisions of Tata Steel Limited. Here, I invite you to join me in a deep dive into various aspects of leadership, teamwork, success, and career lessons while sharing some of the most noteworthy moments of my career.

But hold on! Before we do that, we need to take a pause and discuss some basic concepts – which I am sure some of you might be aware of – of how the operations in the mining area look like.

Let me share some more on the raw materials division before we take a deeper dive into this topic for the benefit of a few readers who might never have worked in steel and mining organizations.

We need to delve a bit into steelmaking and coal mining processes.

The making of steel requires many raw materials, the most prominent of which is coking coal. It's a specific type of coal with a certain percentage of ash in it, which makes it suitable for use in the steelmaking process. Contrary to what many people may believe, coal plays an even more important role in the making of steel by adding its carbon content and other ingredients. Broadly speaking, carbon in coal actually becomes part of iron to make it good quality steel.

There are two types of coal mines – Open-cast and underground. Open-cast mining is a surface mining method used when coal seams are near the surface. Open-cast coal mining recovers a greater proportion of the coal deposit than underground methods, as more of the coal seams in the strata may be exploited. Equipment used in open-cast mining includes draglines, power shovels, large trucks, bucket wheel excavators, and conveyors. Explosives are used to break through the surface or overburden of the mining area. The overburden is not transported to waste dumps for disposal but is cast or hauled directly into adjacent mined out areas for no further use. Open-cast mining is the most economic option for a deposit up to a certain depth where the economic ratio of ore and waste can be sustained. We have an open-cast mine in the raw material division where I spent a larger part of my career.

When the coal is found at greater depth from the surface and it is not economically or otherwise feasible to excavate the entire top layer or overburden, underground mining is the only way. Underground mining is a method of mining that involves the extraction of minerals and ores located deep within the earth's crust. It is used when the deposit is too deep for surface mining or when the terrain is too steep for surface mining to be economical. Underground mining methods include room and pillar, longwall, and block caving. Underground mining is generally more expensive than open-cast mining and is often more hazardous for human beings but has less impact on the environment as it does not lead to the generation of dust and does not require deforestation on the surface.

Raw coal coming out of the open-cast mine has a range of ash percentages. The raw coal is passed through the Coal Handling and Coal Preparation plants during which it is crushed to smaller sizes and separated from rock and soil.

I know it's getting a bit technical, but just stay with me for a few more minutes as it's important to understand these before we get into the story which I actually want to share. Also, this background will pave the path for more chapters in this book.

To resume further, the coal is then transported through conveyor belts and ropeways to a coal washery. The purpose of a coal washery is to reduce the ash content in coal through a mix of segregation, blending, and washing techniques. Coal washing is an integral part of coal production, and it is carried out to reduce the ash content and to lower the level of sulfur and unwanted minerals present in coal. Washed coal has a higher calorific value than unwashed coal; hence the usage of washed coal helps in improving the efficiency of steel, cement, and power plants. A coal washery is a facility that washes coal of soil and rock, crushes it into graded sized chunks (sorting), stockpiles grades preparing it for transport to the market, and more often than not, also loads coal into rail cars, barges, or ships. Clean coal refers to coal that has been treated to reduce its emissions of pollutants such as Sulfur Dioxide and Nitrogen Oxide. The coal particles with higher ash percentages are known as Middling's and Tailings. Middling's are particles of coal that are intermediate in size between those that are washed and those that are not. Tailings are the materials left over after the process of separating the valuable fraction from the uneconomic fraction (gangue) of an ore. In mining, tailings or tails are the materials left over after the process of separating the valuable fraction from the uneconomic fraction (gangue) of coal. In other words, tailings are the coal particles with the highest ash percentages. While clean coal is used in steelmaking after blending it with other coal, Middling's and Tailings are used for other applications including its use as fuel in foundries, thermal power plants, cement factories, and other secondary usages.

Now, we move into the story which I saw unfolding in my life and work in West Bokaro, which was and is an open-cast mining division.

Traditionally, leaders from mines were brought to head collieries but not vice versa. When Mr. B. Muthuraman became the Managing Director, he implemented new practices. One of the new initiatives he implemented was to bring leaders from the steel business to head collieries. This decision was initially viewed with skepticism by certain segments of people. However, it soon became clear that this change in leadership brought in a new way of looking at collieries and a new set of global initiatives.

That was a great example of how bringing in new leaders from an entirely different background could actually bring about new changes and perspectives.

I was working as the head of a quarry in the West Bokaro division during those days. It was the largest quarry in the area. We were producing coking coal with an ash percentage of 15 or 16. Since the ash percentage of the coal was high, it was not used directly for making steel in Jamshedpur. Coal from another division with underground mines was regarded as much better in quality. West Bokaro was seen as a producer of coal suitable for blending with better-grade coal from other sources. Tata Steel had to import much better quality coal from other countries at a much higher cost.

Then, for the first time, the leadership team at West Bokaro decided to do something which was never thought of earlier. First, it was decided to reduce the ash percentage to an unprecedented level of 13.5%, which meant the total coal production was to come down significantly due to improved quality/reduced ash percentage. This meant we had to increase the production of raw coal from quarries so that while reducing the ash percentage, the total quantity of coal did not decrease.

Many initiatives were taken, and finally, the production of coal went up from 1.7 million tons to 2.3 million tons, which was an increase of 35%. Remarkably enough, we achieved this increase while reducing the ash percentage, which would have otherwise brought the production down. Since I was the head of the largest quarry, I had the challenging task of increasing the production of raw coal. We accomplished this in an interesting way.

As they say, necessity is the mother of invention. When we realized that the earlier ways of working were not going to give us the increased production level, we thoroughly reviewed the entire flow plan of the quarry to the washery once again. I remember spending many hours taking rounds of the whole quarry multiple times with the geological planning team. During these travels, we discovered that certain seams of quarries had been exposed but were never used because the ash percentage was high. In other words, these seams consisted of coal of inferior quality. Now that we had to find all ways to enhance coal production, we viewed this seam as an opportunity and held meetings with the processing teams (coal washery) to process this lower-grade raw coal as well. This was a challenging task, but I witnessed one of the best examples of teamwork when the team from other functions understood the genuine need and accepted the challenge to 'wash' or process this lower-grade coal as well.

This was one of the best examples of stretching ourselves to meet extraordinary targets.

We all had to stretch ourselves in a manner people had never practiced in the past. As a result of the reduction in ash percentage of the clean coal, the generation of Middlings and Tailings increased. These are the by-products with higher ash percentages which are unsuitable for use in steel plants but have value in brick kilns, foundries, and many other applications where, technically speaking, heat energy is required.

In essence, because of the reduction in ash percentage, all functions were affected.

The washery teams were affected because they had to handle a higher throughput of raw coal and also handle poorer quality of raw coal.

The secondary products teams were affected because they had to find more customers for selling by-products. Their selling and marketing efforts had to increase.

The quarries were affected because the teams had to excavate extra raw coals to compensate for the reduction in the output of clean coal.

Geological Services are affected because they have to do extra work of doing sampling and analysis of coal. Also, they have to work rather closely with Quarries and Washeries on a day-to-day basis to execute new plans.

Quality and Continuous Improvement departments have to come up with new projects to give boost to new production norms by engaging more people in the new system of *change management.*

Now, we have used the right word – Change Management.

Today, when I reflect back on what we achieved as a team in West Bokaro Division by reducing the percentage of ash of the clean coal, we realize that it was nothing less than a high level change management process.

A division which had never produced clean coal at a lower ash%, was to produce clean coal at an unprecedented low level. This process was to create new challenges for every department and that needed a change management exercise to be implemented in the division. I recall, to help the process, we also had a team from E. Goldratt coming to train us on the Theory of Constraint (TOC). They helped us identify the bottleneck departments in the entire division and that meant some extra work for the employees working in those departments. We had created a core team to work with the TOC team.

This entire exercise involved some very pertinent lessons on leadership and team working. I saw many of these lessons in action in those years. Let me enumerate a few below:

Leadership is all about inspiring teams: Here, a leader who was new to a coal mine, had a fresh outlook toward the business and thought afresh. He filled his team with the inspiration to create a renewed sense of pride and joy to try something new. He gave them a *mantra* of clean coal at 13.5% ash and '13 months' production in 12 months.' That meant giving one month's extra production to the company.

Healthy Competition: There are many raw material sites under Tata Steel Limited. West Bokaro, which is an open cast mine, is one of them. There are other underground mines with a better quality of coal. The leadership team created a sense of pride in the team at West Bokaro by setting a stretched goal with a reward of pride and team benefit in front of them. The leadership focused on the strengths of West Bokaro instead of its weakness. They focused on the fact that the cost of production of coal at West Bokaro was lesser than that at Jamadoba. By enhancing the contribution of West Bokaro coal to steel plant, they could have reduced the overall cost of steel as producing higher volume was always the strength of West Bokaro.

Communication and coordination: Regular communication and coordination sessions were held with Functional heads before and during the process of change management. I recall having been called for so many meetings at Jamshedpur. Also, many regular meetings were held at West Bokaro. These meetings ranged from planning, strategizing, input gathering and conflict resolution to rewards and recognition and celebrating wins.

Guidance and Support: We had consultants from the team of Eliyahu Goldratt working with us for many months. I remember those South African consultants, who were the experts on the Theory of Constraints, working with our teams for many months. They studied the whole system, helped us with the constraints in the systems, made presentations, took the queries of 'doubting Thomases' and convinced them of the genuine need to make some changes in their very own departments. As we all know, people normally want to see faults in others' departments. They do not want to accept that their very own department is in a serious need of transformation.

Rewards & Recognition: As we took this challenging project and worked for extra hours every week – week after week – there were bound to be extra ordinary rewards. Though there were many challenges as well on the way, especially in the initial period. We created many special task forces/teams to complete various projects to debottleneck many areas and enhance production level. As we attained many of these results, award ceremonies were held and people were recognized in the presence of colleagues and superiors thereby adding to their motivation. These award ceremonies were held in a grand way amidst fun and frolic. Also, few employees were promoted based on their exemplary leadership abilities. Some were given special increments and one-time adjustments. These events and happenings led to an increase in energy and motivation level of people and created lot of goodwill and enthusiasm.

"This is yet another example of how changes can be taken as opportunities by looking at them positively and while working with teams in anticipation of a better future."

CHAPTER NINE

Diary of a Maintenance Engineer

Those who are connected to the excellent work culture of Tata group often say, "Once a Tata person, always a Tata person." I strongly believe in this sentiment.

Having spent quite some time in the field of maintenance, you will encounter various stories throughout this diary that reflect my deep association with maintenance work. Therefore, you might also say, "Once a maintenance person, always a maintenance person."

Even in a leadership position, every time I visited a machine workshop or a maintenance site, I felt connected to where I started my journey. Like any true maintenance professional, I could often diagnose machine issues just from the sound, vibrations, or even the smell of oil and lubricants. Extending the lifespan of machines and improving their performance beyond design specifications is both an art and science, requiring a profound love or passion for the vast field of maintenance, which is, of course, a realm of scientific study and deep knowledge.

Now, I would like to share a few learnings based on my journey of Total Quality Management (TQM).

I started my career as a maintenance engineer, and making machines work for longer became a matter of intrigue and deep passion for me. People often use the word "passion" casually, but we all understand its true meaning and value.

It's like a person falling in love with the art of cooking, starting as a novice but evolving into the creator of many authentic and innovative recipes due to their deep passion for the subject. This transformation takes years, eventually turning the individual into a figure like Tarla Dalal or someone else in their culinary domain.

Similarly, a cricketer begins by simply hitting a ball but gradually learns the finer details of the game—the necessary fitness to run between wickets, the power required to hit or bowl, the art of swing bowling, and how line and length affect the game. With time and practice, these details become second nature, enabling the cricketer to execute a perfect yorker or hit a six effortlessly, almost without conscious thought. It becomes natural.

The same progress applies to a painter, athlete, writer, leader, speaker, and so on.

It was the same with me as a maintenance engineer. My passion was not only limited to the intricacies of machines but also to other subjects closely or distantly related to the field of maintenance.

Total Productive Maintenance (TPM) is one such field related to maintenance. Another field related to maintenance is Total Quality Management (TQM), commonly known by its acronym—TQM.

I still remember a case study from the field of TQM that I would like to share for the benefit of readers. It illustrates how, by following a stepwise process, one can improve productivity on the shop floor. Well, maybe you can also apply this principle elsewhere in other aspects of life.

The case study goes like this.

A Piston Ring manufacturing plant had its own casting (Iron) plant. The castings produced were used to manufacture piston rings. While manufacturing rings, it was observed that 20% of casts produced were rejected while machining it.

This was significantly higher than the average rate of rejection in any casting or foundry factory which hovers around 3-4%.

A TQM expert was called to study and make recommendations to improve the quality of castings/ foundry which in other words meant – to reduce the rejection rate.

First thing which the expert did was to closely monitor the working environment and processes in the plant. There were four operators doing the casting work and he found that one of them, James, had a different way of working than the remaining three foundrymen.

Before starting his work in the beginning of the shift, James had the habit of cleaning old pieces of molten metal from earlier castings stuck to the inner wall of the crucible. He used to start fresh castings only after having cleaned the remains of metal pieces left from older castings.

It was found that the rejection rate in his case was as low as 7-8% which was still high as compared to the standard rate of rejection but it was still much lower than the rate of rejection in case of other operators who used to have a rejection % higher than 20%, say in the range of 20-25%. When taken as an average, the rejection stood at around 15-18%.

This is where the first action came - other operators were trained to practice what James did i.e., to clean old pieces of metal. A Standard Operating Procedure or SOP was also prepared and shared with other operators. This reduced the rejection rate to around 10-12%.

However, the target was 3-4%. So, what else could have been done to achieve the goal?

Inspired by this early win, the TQM expert broke the entire process of casting into five different elements including preparation of sand casting, heating of metal, pouring of molten metal, etc. They studied the entire chain while looking at each 'link' individually and minutely. Process anomalies were identified at each stage and operators were trained to upgrade the process at various stages. One of the anomalies discovered was – the amount of molten metal poured by each operator varied. Some operators poured more molten metal and others poured less metal than the needed quantity.

They marked an optimum level to which molten metal was to be poured in the crucible. Now, each operator was pouring the exact quantity of molten metal and this process improvement led to the rejection rate coming down to 3-4%.

Now they were operating at the standard rate of rejection level. To hold the gains, they developed a plan for formalizing SOPs thru training and certification process for managers and casters.

If you reflect back on the process followed, you will realize that Total Quality Management as a process can be applied to any field of life to make improvements and reduce undesired outcomes.

You need to observe, study the process, train people, and document the process.

Related to this, there is another learning which I am sharing for the benefit of the readers. I came across this in one of the management development programs.

This is the real story of older days where typewriters were used for typing work. It was the pre-computer era. A company had twelve typewriters and an annual maintenance contract for the typewriters. However, they were facing a problem with poor typing quality; some of the letters were faint in color. After careful study, they discovered that one of the twelve typists was experiencing issues with typing quality. Some of the letters were not appearing with the desired quality. They decided to talk to the typist.

When questioned, the typist denied committing any negligence.

Upon inspecting the machine, they found that a few letters on the typewriter were not making proper impressions; the impressions were faint. Further investigation revealed that the movement of a letter arm corresponding to the press of the button was smaller than required. This was because these letters were used more frequently in the text than others, causing their settings to change noticeably. As a result, these letters required more frequent adjustment than others.

The company modified the standard operating procedure (SOP), and they never encountered the problem of poor typing quality again.

In this case, the problem did not lie with the operator but with the machine. However, people—generally speaking—tend to judge and blame individuals for any mistake without investigating the root causes.

The fault can lie with people, machines, or processes. Instead of blaming individuals, let's pause and identify where the cause of the problem lies.

Another case study from a company reveals an interesting story about the connection between breakdown maintenance and retention of talent. The company used to believe in hiring and firing employees who did not meet the expected level of availability. However, they discovered that this practice led to higher breakdown costs, ultimately increasing overall expenses. The cost of breakdown maintenance exceeded the cost of hiring and firing employees. Essentially, if the company focused on preventive maintenance and adhered to processes, they incurred lower costs compared to the expenses associated with hiring and firing.

We can draw a parallel from sports here.

In Cricket, everyone knows Mahendra Singh Dhoni, who maintains that winning and losing are part of the game, but following the process and maintaining discipline—both physically and emotionally—is within our control. By taking care of the process and proactively following it, we can avoid losses.

In all these examples, we are talking about maintaining the process and being proactive. We are discussing doing a proper analysis of the root cause behind undesired outcomes or failures. We are talking about being consistent with the process of analysis and taking actions rather than being swayed by things or symptoms which are too obvious to be true.

There are applications of these examples in real life as well. For example, you might have seen that people who ensure proper maintenance of their car do not face any trouble for longer. People not only need to take care of scheduled maintenance of the car but also should maintain the optimum tire pressure for smooth running and optimum fuel consumption.

"If you can, do some study of the principles of TQM and apply these in your own life and work. You will be happily surprised at the positive outcomes. It's a connected world after all."

CHAPTER TEN

Across Different Generations

I started my career as a maintenance engineer before I came to the field of operations.

As a maintenance engineer, I often used to come across many challenges related to enhancement of uptime and availability of machines. For the uninitiated, let me write a bit about the kind of machines which one encounters in a colliery.

For the breaking of overburden layers, you need drilling machines and 'charging' machines. These machines make holes in layers of overburden and fill these holes with explosives before causing controlled explosion to loosen rock pieces. Then, Rear Dumpers (a type of heavy earth moving machines) are engaged to carry the rocks away to a separate dump yard. Once the coal seam is exposed, again drilling, and charging operations are replicated, this time to loosen the coal pieces. Now, Bottom Dumpers, another type of heavy earth moving machines, are engaged to carry coal from the coal mine to the coal handling plant. Excavators are used to load rock and debris on rear dumpers and coal onto the bottom dumpers.

In coal handling plants, there are separate set of machines including coal crushers, conveyors, and ropeways, etc. Then we have a host of machines in coal washeries.

Here, we will keep our conversation limited to the machines in collieries. Their uptime or available hours is crucial. As a maintenance in charge, it was my duty to see that the machines are available for maximum possible time. A machine's availability is affected by predictive and planned maintenance as well as breakdown maintenance. Many a times in my career, I used to be challenged in both humble and aggressive tones to enhance the availability or uptime of machines.

I always believed in a practice which I would like to share here for the evaluation by readers.

When challenged, always keep your focus on planned and corrective work. Never – beyond a point – waste your energy on justifying or unnecessarily clarifying your stance to people. If you spend too much time in saying all that you are going to do, you will give an impression of being defensive. Your focus will be lifted off from the main area of work. Instead, get outcomes and show to people.

I always put my focus on analyzing the downtime and its reasons, choosing the most important preventive and corrective actions, motivating my maintenance team to do their duty, guiding them if needed, and also pulling them up if they showed lack of energy in doing what was needed. Once we take accountability for outcomes, everything else fits in place.

Showing results instead of explaining is important because it provides the user with a visual representation of what they are looking for. It also helps the user to quickly identify the information they need without having to listen through time-consuming explanations and stories. This is especially important when the user is looking for specific information and needs to find it quickly.

People always look for results and do not really care for the efforts or work which you do in between.

Don't *say* to them, *show* them – this is one mantra which will do a lot better for you than making promises and failing to keep them.

In my journey of life and career, I have come across many situations and based on my personal and deep experiences, I would like to share a few lessons which I believe every corporate professional must keep in mind.

Here are a few points for the readers to consider and reflect on:

1. Every organization has a certain way of working and certain expectations from people. It has a unique way of responding to the same set of stimulants. This unique organizational trait is known as organizational culture. It depends on various factors. It depends on the leaders who have led the organization and left their footprints along their journey of leadership. It depends on the values which the organization has set for itself. It also depends on the priorities which the organization keeps its focus on. Initially, certain leaders shape the culture and then the organizational culture begins to shape the behaviors of employees. It's an interesting relationship – isn't it?

   For a professional to succeed in their career, it's important that their individual traits match with the traits of the organization. It's important that people understand the culture of the organization and modify their way of working to suit the culture. Even extremely good performers may be failures if they join an organization whose culture they can't fit into. In extreme and rare cases, if you feel that fitment to the culture is against your principles, unfortunately, the only way ahead for you is out of the organization.

2. You can't stop the organization culture from changing. The culture changes with time depending on the current leader and priorities

arising due to external and internal factors. It's important to understand the changes and adjust one's priorities as per the changing priorities of the organization.

3. One must be able to gauge the changing priorities of stakeholders. You must know who your stakeholders are and what they are looking for from you. If you fail to understand the specific needs of various stakeholders including leaders, peers, team members, government agencies, and villagers, for example, you will not be able to address specific needs and priorities and will fail to make a deeper connection and impression. To cite an example, suppose you work under a leader who stays focused on outcomes and results, you can't succeed while just talking about your efforts. In such a background, say less and let the results speak for themselves. Just report the outcomes and before that, if you need support from the manager, just speak about those. On the contrary, if you have a manager who is a coach and mentor and loves to discuss your personal and professional life thereby providing guidance and advice, you can take liberty and share more on your efforts and endeavors. Outcomes would still be crucial but you can share more and converse with the manager as you undertake a project.

This is yet another story on change management.

"We all know that change is a way of life. I have a few pointers on this. I would advise the readers to meditate over the three sentences shared below and build these in life. The pointers are as follows:

If changes are inevitable, why not to change?

Who should change? Why not I?

When to change? Why not Now?"

CHAPTER ELEVEN

Eight Laws of Power

Many youngsters come to the corporate world thinking that it's all going to be rosy and as per the lessons and theories taught in management books. But in reality, some new forces come to play and hence there is a separate chapter on 'Power and Politics' in all books on Organizational Behavior. Let me share my take on this important topic.

Once I was fortunate to have been nominated for a residential training program in Tata Management Training Center (TMTC) in the early days of my joining Tata Steel at West Bokaro. The training program, titled as 'Interpersonal effectiveness for technical managers,' was basically designed while keeping the need of engineers in mind who were fresh from colleges but did not understand power and politics in corporate set up. Also, they did not know how to work with people and build a positive, productive and conducive working relationships.

I would like to talk about some of the lessons which I learned and later used in my working life. It was one of the most life defining training programs which I have ever attended and I actually absorbed most of what had been taught. When today I see people taking their training programs lightly and looking at them just as a mean to get a certificate which they can flaunt to get career progressions, I am reminded of the need of actual and deep learning and not one which is just on the face value.

One of the sessions at TMTC was on the 'eight different types of power' which people exude in real life. Power is the capacity or ability to direct or influence the behavior of others or the course of events. Different types of power are as follows:

1. Information power
2. Reference power
3. Reward & recognition power
4. Coercive power
5. Legitimate power
6. Moral & Ethical power
7. Commitment power
8. Expert power

Briefly speaking, people gain power by either one or a combination of more than one of these attributes.

Let me say a bit about each of these, and you can connect from your own life as we progress.

People who have knowledge of certain things which others do not have wield power. But this is short-term as they lose the power the moment they share their knowledge. This explains why some people in organizations are keen on knowing what is happening around them and are keen on holding power to themselves.

People who have connections and know individuals who can bring value or influence things and decisions wield power through reference. They are connected to someone powerful and hence benefit from the rub-off effect of power. For example, a relative of the promoter of a company will wield this type of power within the company, and you can't deny this.

A person who is in a position to reward or recognize others will have this power, as they can influence the behavior of people by giving them benefits. A Managing Director of a company will have this power as they can choose certain people for annual increments and benefits, thereby keeping them aligned.

Power also comes to some by instilling fear and threatening others with adverse consequences. The fear of reprimand, job loss, or financial consequences makes people align with a certain person. It may be surprising, but a few leaders still believe in controlling others using coercive power. Whether liked or not, there are people who use this power over others.

Legitimate power comes from the position you hold. A CEO can affect someone's career by virtue of the power given to them due to their position.

Moral and ethical power is the most long-lasting and desired form of power because you command respect due to your moral and ethical conduct. A leader who is seen as an ideal and inspiring figure will always be respected and wield influence even if they do not seek it.

Commitment has been described as 'dedication, steadfastness, allegiance, faithfulness, and loyalty to a cause or goal.' It's about giving oneself to a cause with success as the only option. Commitment binds you irrevocably to a cause you believe in until success comes. Therefore, your commitment also gives you power.

Expert power is a type of power that comes from having a high level of knowledge within your area of expertise. Expert power is relative. This means that if two people have varying levels of knowledge on a subject, the one with more knowledge has expert power.

Later in my career and life, I saw the application of each type of power while coming across various people, and this helped me a lot in making the right decisions.

Let me share a few stories of how I personally experienced a few of these types. I am sure, as you read through, you can also connect these stories with your life and experiences.

When someone else was selected for the position in Jamadoba, it's an example of power by reference and also positional power.

People should avoid commenting on sensitive matters in public. Someone who is 'close to the power' may share all of these to use against you. Hence, be wary of saying something negative in public. If you say something positive about someone else – who is not in the 'hall' – the good words may not reach the person. But if you say something negative about someone or participate in gossip against the person, in all likelihood, the words will reach the person who is not expected to hear these. This is simply because people are extra excited to spread something which is sensitive or provocative. Goodness is slow to spread, and negative news spreads faster.

Hence, build habits to keep confidentiality and abstain from indulging in gossip. It could be a career saver for you.

One important thing about ethical power is – you are honest but you must also appear to be honest.

You should constantly look for ways on how to improve knowledge and become the expert on the subject. This gives you the power due to knowledge.

Related to the topic of power and politics is the subject of taking some tough decisions even if there is a bit of resistance. You should not give in just because there is power and politics around you. These will continue to be there and while you should keep safe, you should also not let rule your life and career decisions.

Though everyone faces different circumstances in their career based on which they take their decisions, I always have gone with my gut feeling taking life and career decisions. If I felt it was wrong, I spoke for this even if this required courage and discomfort on the way. Sooner or later – maybe with some unpleasant developments in the way – with persistence, I always got what I wanted.

Examples could be many.

I remember one instance when three of my colleagues who were thought to be closer to the people in power, appeared for an interview for a few vacant positions along with me and my colleagues got selected where I was not. One of the reasons for this was that the positions were pertaining to underground mines which was none of my interest.

I have always been very clear about my priorities and trivialities. Also, I have been clear about my likes and dislikes. For me, there were no gray zones in life, most of the time.

This clarity of purpose also extended to the type of mines I wanted to work in.

I always wanted to work in open-cast mines and wanted to build my career in this field of mining. I was never inclined toward working in an underground mine.

Tata Steel had both underground and open-cast mines in different locations in the same state, and rotation of people between the places was pretty common. Many people were being transferred from one location to another and that also meant that people worked in both types of mines intermittently. However, both were entirely different working experiences.

In open-cast mining, you can see the whole of the mine while standing atop a cliff on the edge. You can see the mine below and the sun above your head. In an underground mine, it's dark and dreary as you descend through a vertical tunnel into endless depths. It's a pretty much different and darker experience.

Many of my colleagues who started their career with open-cast mines shifted to underground mines looking for promotional opportunities. They often could never come back to an open-cast mine as their experience became their baggage which kept pulling them behind. But as I said, there were hardly any gray zones for me in life. My priorities and preferences were clear. For the sake of a promotion, I never abandoned my preference in this field as well.

During the interview, when a senior leader on the panel asked me a question about underground mines, I made it clear that while I wouldn't mind answering technical questions related to underground mining, I would never actually like to work in an underground mine. Instead, I would like to build my career in an open-cast mine as I thought I could add more value there and had already built a rich and long experience on which I wanted to build further and do some meaningful job for the company.

The panelists were surprised to hear this. Maybe my forthrightness did not go down well with them as they probably were not prepared for such a response.

Courage is often unlikable in our society, and the corporate world is no exception. There was indeed an iota of courage in my reply. I am not sure if it could also have been construed as 'arrogance' by a few panelists. In my opinion, I was not inflexible. I was just being forthright and true as I had a vivid picture in my mind of where and how I wanted to shape my career.

So, was I selected for the position?

Well, your premonition is right.

I was not considered any further for that promotional opportunity.

That was one of the first promotional interviews of my career, and I was heartbroken. It often happens that when we have not experienced failure, it hits us harder. As we 'mature' in life, we start taking these with less hurt and actually also use some rejections or failures to our advantage. In fact, I do know people who have become successful primarily because of rejections which made them think differently and do what they otherwise have not done. Bill Gates also has said – "Success is a lousy teacher. It seduces smart people into thinking that they can't lose."

Of course, I was too young then to understand this. Like many young people, all that I wanted was a promotion letter. Rest all was meaningless.

Of course, while speaking with the panelists, I did not realize that being forthright and candid could bring pain. It took me some time before I realized how hurtful a feeling losing a chance of career ascendance could be, especially at that young age.

I took a break for more than a month and went on leave to my village. It was too long a break from even the regular standards of those days but I just wanted to live with my father for some time. This also helped me come out of my temporary grief and frustration from one of my first 'losses.'

My father was the main source of my inspiration, and as I have said elsewhere in the book, it was one step of courage on his part – when he left his village to study and do a job elsewhere – which shaped a brighter destiny for me and forthcoming generations. When in doubt and dejection, he was my go-to person.

I was seeking a lesson or two – among other lessons and learnings – on how to make courage work in one's favor, if at all one could.

"I would strongly recommend that readers look at power as an essential tool to make good things happen. Just because a few negative people use power for undesired outcomes does not take the sheen from the word power. Good people use power to implement good practices by influencing others. Study power, connect the dots with your own life, and use it for good reasons."

CHAPTER TWELVE

Missed Opportunities

I have been privileged to visit many countries.

My visit to Australia gave me an important insight which every reader should pay attention to. There, after working in an organization for a few years, every employee - Leader, Manager, or team member - has to take a sabbatical to study in a university and rejoin. This is mandatory for seeking continuance, promotions, and career ascendance. Learning during a sabbatical is like a ticket for further working in the organization. Knowledge is combined with education at the university. If you do not upgrade, your next-level ticket is not available.

I found this to be a great idea and would strongly recommend to every reader also to take a pause and ask this question to self - Are you also learning and upgrading yourself?

While attending some of the sessions in the Australian university, I realized another important thing - Most of us in Indian culture hesitate to ask questions. We have a certain degree of inhibition to be extra courteous and polite to the extent that we don't even ask questions despite being willing to do so. We had many students from various countries, and I hardly saw anyone hesitating before asking. It was a two-way conversation which brought out the best learning and lessons.

Asking is such an important aspect of learning and growth. Be respectful but ask. Tony Robbins, the famous motivational speaker, says that you can attain anything in the world provided you follow the following three steps: Ask, Ask the right person, and keep asking till you get it!

Success is as simple – and it does not mean it's easy – as it sounds and it begins with one simple concept – Ask!

I have also visited the USA, China, Singapore, and Thailand and gained new insights from each visit.

I remember having attended a conference in Thailand. It was so useful for the simple fact that otherwise, people work in silos within their own teams or their own locations. Once in a while, to attend these conferences, people come together and learn from each other. They also make new friends and renew their bonds. They, in other words, expand their horizons of learning, networking, and being more valuable to the company.

I also distinctly remember my visit to Mozambique. The experience was 'different' right from the time I landed at the airport. I saw a unique practice there. As your bags come out of the airport on a conveyor belt, you will notice local people, not even authorized by the airport authority, coming to pick up your bags and keep them in a trolley. But the intention is not to steal. It is to ask for some money after carrying your bags from the conveyor belt to your cab. I remember one of the neighboring passengers telling me softly – "Don't worry. He will take your bags to the car and you can give some money. It's a normal practice here..."

I realized how poverty-stricken people are in different parts of the world and especially in the African continent. People did not have employment or money. There was not much available as a source of their livelihood. There were some rich people as well but the disparity was obvious and visible everywhere. I could see tall buildings and shanty hutments co-existing on both sides of the street as I drove to the mining area which I had come to visit.

When I reached the mining site, I found it impressive. Africa is known for its rich possession of minerals and metals. I saw beautiful site management conditions there which we later adopted.

During the visit, I closely watched how people used to do the mining work there and faced difficulties on the way.

Their biggest difficulty was logistics. Africa is a large continent, and hence laying an integrated network of roads, railheads, and waterways was a necessary requirement of mine planning.

The nearest railhead was far from the site. Hence, they used to first transport the coal through dumpers which carried coal to the railhead. From there, the coal was transported to the riverbed and subsequently loaded onto cargo ships.

Hence, in Mozambique, transportation of coal involved trucks, rail, river cruises, and ships, which led to a very high cost of transportation and logistics.

You might have noted that I have mentioned 'missed opportunities' in the headline of this chapter. You might be wondering how international travels are linked to missed opportunities.

There is a crucial point here for all the readers – especially for the generations of today and tomorrow – to grow in their career and life and make a wider impact on society.

I realized how poverty-stricken people are in different parts of the world and especially in the African continent. People did not have employment or money. There was not much available as a source of their livelihood. There were some rich people as well but the disparity was obvious and visible everywhere. I could see tall buildings and shanty hutments co-existing on both sides of the street as I drove to the mining area which I had come to visit.

Let me take a step back and tell you that I had made the trip to Africa with the approval of the then senior leader of Tata Steel, his deputy who was from the senior leadership team of raw materials division, and another leader from the strategy department in the company. They were like mentors to me, and as it often happens, you feel a little too courteous with your mentors. I also was no exception. After my return, I submitted the report to my immediate superior and did not make any efforts to make a presentation to the senior leader whom my manager used to report to. Maybe I could have proposed to my manager to book a time slot with the senior leader for a presentation. The senior leader would surely have agreed. In fact, I later came to know that he was a little disappointed that no one took efforts to present the findings to him and talk about the practices which could have been implemented in Tata Steel. But this did not happen.

I guess the senior leader might have received a brief and casual update about my visit from my manager, but nothing moved beyond this. Had I made a formal presentation after formally seeking a time slot in the presence of the senior leader who could have invited other experts for the meeting, the outcome could have been different. I could have explained things from my first-hand experience which is always more crucial. A good example of first-hand experience could be a Head of Operations listening to a serious machine-related problem from a mechanic working on the shop floor rather than hearing it from the line manager. A workman's version would be more enriching as he would be speaking from his personal experiences.

Then one day, I was in the office of the same senior leader for another meeting and he suddenly asked me why I did not present my findings to him. I tried saying something but I could see that he was unhappy as he heard me briefly and moved for another meeting.

That day I realized how our lack of conviction and courage – laced with our over willingness to be courteous and follow hierarchical restrictions – can keep potential opportunities away from us.

It was evident that I had missed the opportunity to directly convey the lessons from my visit to the MD which actually could have made him advise other project heads to implement some of the best practices based on my learnings. He could have advised other leaders to speak with me and put ideas into practice.

But none of these could happen because I submitted the report to my Manager and did not ask for an opportunity to make a presentation before senior leaders.

In summary, I did not 'Ask.' I stayed silent and thought my duty was over with sending a report to my manager.

It's the same point which we also covered in a slightly different context while talking about my education in Australian universities.

Had I 'asked,' I could have presented to the senior leader in a better way. He would have got a better insight. He could have made some better decisions. Also, after seeing more value in my visits, I could have been asked to visit more mines in more continents and I could have become more valuable for the company.

Let me cite another example to illustrate this point. I still remember the day when I received the news of being selected as one of the delegates of 'India Mining Mission.' The delegation had senior people including the 'Secretary of Mines & Development' and Chairman of the Confederation of Indian Industries (CII) as its members.

As a member of the delegation, I visited nickel mines in Canada. For the first time, I saw large machines similar to coal haulers being used at a depth of 5,000 feet. In India, coal haulers are used only in open-cast mines at a shallow depth of 50-100 feet. The usage of coal haulers in underground mines at such high depths was a revelation to us.

After visiting the mines, we moved to Toronto and Montreal, where the head office of the company hosting us was located. While talking to the officials of the company, I came to know of the political situation and the social conditions there. I understood how the mining companies had a clearly defined responsibility of protecting and serving the rights of the aborigines. There were clear laws and regulations for providing support to the aborigines. They had taken the concept of Corporate Social Responsibility to a new level. They had to give a certain percentage of their profits to the aborigines. All of this was done to compensate people for their land which had been acquired by the company.

In the mining company we visited, people had to work in mining for around 4 months and then engage in transportation of coal for the remaining 8 months. They used to stock the raw material for 4 months. Then, during the remaining 8 months, they used to convert the stock into concentrate and transfer it to the nearby railhead. The nickel ore had to be transported through a pipe conveyor system to the nearby railhead. To ensure that the concentrate flow did not solidify on the way, it was surrounded by a continuous flow of hot steam. It was a great technological breakthrough that impressed me.

Later, I also visited iron ore mines in Brazil, where the ore was transported from the Brazilian port to the UK.

After each of these visits, I did not request time from the Managing Director (MD) to make a presentation on the findings and suggestions that we could implement in Tata Steel. I simply sent the report to my superior and did not check whether he would like us to make a presentation to the MD as well.

Today, when I reflect, I think I could not make these presentations for a variety of reasons, but ultimately, it was my mistake, and it's something I could have addressed. People around us are busy with their own priorities, and we have to take the lead to act on things we feel convinced about. It's true that in our prevailing work culture, people like to maintain cordial relationships and avoid causing awkward situations like asking one's manager to speak to their manager to seek time for presentations. Our culture—as I mentioned in one of the preceding chapters—is all about not asking too many unnecessary questions. But if you think something is important, not only for you but also for your superior and the company, you will find a way to be humble yet make an important point. It's also true that many large organizations in India are known for their hierarchical structure, where bypassing one's superior is not encouraged. Your job is to present to your superior and leave it at that. I respected my superiors and enjoyed working under their leadership. I am mentioning this to highlight the cultural fabric in which we work. However, you should not let it become an impediment for the company. You can develop your own communication and influencing skills to better manage upward communication. Additionally, though this is not the deciding criteria, if you get a great manager, consider yourself lucky. I have been fortunate to have some really great managers, and I am grateful to all of them.

I think you can connect with the points mentioned above.

I think I missed out on opportunities by remaining subdued.

If you come across a similar situation, you should consider speaking with your manager respectfully and humbly to see if you both could team up to create and present a beneficial report for your organization. I think if your intent is right, your manager may also support you.

It's not that I didn't learn from some of these experiences. Realizing that I had to take a bit of risk, I often stuck my neck out to make things happen. Once, I remember, I had to propose a scheme for a coal washery project. My superior was unsure of the outcome. I was confident though and hence requested my superior to let me go ahead, taking full accountability for its success or failure. I got his signature on the papers, accepting complete accountability. Initially, I almost had to force him to sign the papers, but later on, the project's success was so good that my superior sent me a congratulatory note.

The message here is—once in a while, we have to stick our neck out and stand for what we truly believe in. Success does not come easily.

On two occasions, I received an offer from another Indian MNC for a substantial salary to lead international projects. I was nearing my superannuation in Tata Steel then and was worried about gratuity and retirement dues, etc., despite knowing that the compensation offered for international postings would have been more than enough to cover any outstanding dues. Also, I would have had an extended source of handsome earnings for many years if I had accepted the offer and moved to Mozambique. But I could not muster the courage to take that risk and stayed back. It was like stepping back from leading a global life with good money and a long-term gainful engagement. This is another example of how I missed some important opportunities. I had this opportunity in my hands but could not accept it due to inhibitions, etc. My mind and heart were still with Tata Steel. Had I taken the step, I could have easily been compensated for the loss of some retirement payments. Also, I would have been engaged much longer even after the formal age of retirement. But again, due to my hesitation to take a courageous action, I missed this opportunity as well.

"This is a classic example of how and why we often become our biggest enemy by not unleashing our full potential.

I would like the readers to take a pause and write down 4-5 occasions when opportunities knocked on the door and they could not muster the courage to open the door and move forward.

Also, you may like to introspect after this exercise whether you could have done something differently to make it better.

Chances are, you will realize—when it comes to success in any field, it's mostly about us and less about others."

CHAPTER THIRTEEN

Grandparenting

I have undergone the experience of parenting – which is a very important and unfortunately often a neglected subject – very closely at two different phases in life.

In the first instance, I was the parent of two lovely kids as they grew to be successful professionals themselves.

Then I saw my children playing the role of parents themselves.

The ongoing journey of parenting – and then grandparenting – has been fulfilling, and it also holds a few lessons which I would like to share here in anticipation of readers benefiting from these experiences.

Over the last few decades, I have seen the concept of parenting evolve. The way our parents looked after us was different from the way today's parents take care of their children.

The fact is – we do not treat our kids the way our parents did.

Our parents took care of us while following the tenets of discipline. Also, respect and fear were important ways of parenting for them. They expected their children to respect them, and they did not refrain from instilling a bit of fear to ensure their children did not follow a path of self-destruction.

In essence, parents from the baby boomers' generation were protective of their children and cared about their behavior and success first as students and then as 'would-be responsible citizens.'

Today's kids may be baffled at the thought, but in earlier days, it was acceptable for some parents and teachers to use sticks to discipline their wards. Though I don't think anyone will ever agree that beating or caning is an effective way to teach children important lessons of discipline, focus, and adherence to life's rules. I am not sure, but it might have worked for a few parents and teachers in the bygone era, otherwise why would they have practiced it so vehemently?

This reminds me of one of the teachers in my school who used to carry a thin stick to ensure that students did not venture out of their classrooms and wander in the lobby during class breaks. The 'stick principle' did 'stick on the wall' as the entire lobby used to wear a deserted look during those class breaks.

One of my friends once said that his father used to keep a stick made of a piece of plastic water pipe. The 'stick' was always kept on a rack in a way that the kids could see the pipe as a reminder of the beating they might undergo if they misbehaved. For example, one of the siblings used to often skip classes to go watch a movie in a nearby theater with some rowdy friends. When the father found out, the stick came into play and the severe beating ensured that the other siblings did not repeat the mistake, and even the undisciplined child took enough care not to repeat.

Such a way of controlling behavior is known as corporal punishment.

Surprisingly, this is still used as a way of punishing children in many parts of the world, and one can verify this by searching online. Although it shows a lack of effectiveness and self-control on the part of the parent, and even in places where it is practiced, people agree that it does not work in the longer scheme of things.

So, generally speaking, this was the way of parenting from the annals of history.

Today, the concept of parenting has completely changed.

As we grew, corporal punishment or thrashing gradually took a back seat. We had a good education and understanding from reading newspapers and engaging with social media. People could easily see the prevalent best practices of parenting in some developed countries. With the world becoming more transparent, people realized that the older way of parenting was not the right approach.

Children also became more aware of how kids around the world enjoy privileges like autonomy, safety, and empowerment. They also knew their rights well, thanks to the positive impact of social media.

I often meet my grandparents in Delhi and the USA. I must admit that it is from them that I have been learning the best way of parenting.

My grandchildren in the USA attend classes that even parents of yesterday could never have attended. They participate in swimming, dancing, nature trails, and public speaking classes – just to name a few. Even at a very young age, my grandchildren are almost self-dependent. There is a fundamental requirement in foreign countries. After the age of 15 years, children need to become independent. They should earn and maintain themselves and continue their studies.

When I went to Germany in the 1990s, one of the Indian friends I met there used to work in the evening hours in a nearby restaurant to earn money and take care of his study-related expenses.

Hence, the role of a parent in western countries often concludes when the child turns 15 years old or so. This marks a major shift from India, where parents often support their children's higher studies until they are 25 years old or older.

During my visits to the USA, I have seen that my daughter has been parenting her kids really well. She gives them the freedom to attend various classes and have their own friend circle, but very wisely, she also maintains certain control over their behavior. For example, the kids have been given a phone, but there is a limit on data usage. I find my daughter to be an impressive parent and always find something to learn from her style of parenting.

Today, if you do not expose your children to different aspects of life – like making more friends, playing sports, and working on their personality development – they may struggle in their life later on.

Today's kids are watching programs like Peppa Pig from a very early age and they see how respectfully Peppa's parents are treating their children. They see how Peppa's parents play with children like friends. There is no forcing or causing fear in the minds of children. Peppa's parents explain and convince kids about the right way of learning and living rather than forcing and dictating. Children, in their subconscious mind, create a picture of how their parents should treat them, from the age of nursery and pre-nursery.

I have experienced this while being in the USA – Children in the USA are not happy if they find their parents or grandparents yelling to guide them. They will start reminding the parents politely – "You are yelling at me...!" This is because of the society in which they live, programs which they watch on screens, and behavior which they see being practiced by their friends living in the neighborhood.

Psycho-generational behavior of kids has changed, and parents of today must remember this.

There is also a need for kids to be better prepared for the upcoming intense competition. Today's children are competing against kids from different countries. In earlier days, competition was limited to neighboring kids. Now, kids attend online classes and participate in classes with kids from different places and cultures.

In India, we often spend time with our son and his family. I see that when my wife forces my grandchild to eat, he will not eat. But when we leave the kid alone for a couple of minutes and then advise him to eat, he happily begins to eat. In fact, if you force them, kids will also show you a defiant look and make faces in anger. Remember the angry expressions Ishaan made in the movie 'Taare Zameen Par' every time his parents pushed him into doing something he did not want. But he started opening up once he had a teacher who understood and supported him in his studies and games.

So, in a nutshell, 'physical discipline' or corporal punishment has surely vanished now.

Even 'psychological discipline,' which involved practices like withdrawal of love for some time, shaming, insulting, shouting, or other forms of emotional manipulation, is on the decline, though these have not vanished completely. Recent research findings show that about 72 per cent of parents used such psychological approaches frequently over the past year.

'Non-physical discipline,' which included practices such as reasoning, demonstrating by setting a personal example, or offering children something else (better) to do as an alternative to undesired behavior, often yielded more productive outcomes.

I hope the readers will do some more research on the topic of parenting and reflect on their own behavior while parenting – or even grandparenting – their children.

This is the sole aim behind writing this chapter.

CHAPTER FOURTEEN

Giving Where It Came From

After retiring from my service at Tata Steel Limited, I thought of pursuing my dream of giving back to society in many ways.

Let me explain…

For a long time, I had the purpose of helping people develop skills that would make them employable in their subsequent years of life. A skill that would enable them to support their families and provide good education to their kids, ultimately making the world a better place to live.

While working as the head of maintenance in mining locations, I was deeply involved in the process of hiring permanent as well as contractual laborers and training them on various skill sets. We trained people on maintenance and operation of various types of machines, which subsequently helped them gain permanent employment.

Hence, when I got an opportunity to use this experience and knowledge of mine to make as many people as possible employable, I started a new company with one of my partners. We brainstormed and developed the mission and vision statements of the company.

We started the new company in Jamshedpur, a city known for its many ancillary units of Tata Steel and Tata Motors. There are hundreds of small and medium enterprises requiring thousands of employable youths. Our goal was to train these unemployed youth on various skills and help them secure jobs to support their families for decades to come.

We set up a joint venture with 'Quivan Skill Empowerment Pvt. Ltd.' (QSEPL), Kolkata, which was registered with the National Skill Development Corporation (NSDC). QSEPL received orders from NSDC and outsourced projects to us. We provided the actual skill-based training to the candidates, but their certification was done by QSEPL as they were the authorized entity by NSDC to issue certificates.

The project required a significant investment, which my partner and I made. Over a few years, we trained hundreds of candidates, which was a fulfilling experience for us. We provided training in various skills, including fitting, welding, electrical work, and plumbing, among others.

Apart from providing the final certificates, we handled almost all other aspects of running the project, including marketing campaigns, arranging locations, providing infrastructure, setting up test stations, and liaising with local government agencies. Additionally, we ensured the placement of candidates after their certification.

All these activities kept me as engaged as I was while at Tata Steel.

Looking back on this initiative, I realize that the beginning was not easy. As they say, "a journey of a thousand miles begins with a single step," and the initial steps are always the most difficult. However, if you persist – and this is the most challenging phase – it becomes easier later on.

The first step was to find a senior partner. For those unfamiliar with this process, finding the right partner who shares the same values and vision is a tough task, and one should not rush or compromise, as it may pose bigger challenges later.

I also made a mistake in choosing the partner, which later affected the venture. My advice is – if you want to 'save nine,' a 'stitch in time' is important. This 'stitch' is in the form of conducting due diligence and selecting the right partner. If you invest time in meeting people and choosing the right partner, it will be beneficial in your journey later on.

The next step was to create a webpage for the new entity. The company's webpage outlined four to five pillars, including – but not limited to – the following:

- Training young individuals and providing them with skills (e.g., mechanical, plumbing, welding, etc.).
- Documenting the training process and informing companies about candidates ready for internships. Our message to companies was clear – these candidates understand all the theoretical aspects of welding, plumbing, etc. They are familiar with different voltages and the welding process. They require three months of training during which they can work as assistants to further develop their skills. They will not perform independent work during this period but will assist and learn, preparing them for independent work later on. This approach aligned with the National Skill Development Corporation's guidelines. Initially, we approached companies for training and then for employment, dividing the process into two engaging phases.

I reflect on those four years with nostalgia, which actually started on a pretty inspiring note. I remember the days when we used to do marketing by using posters on vehicles.

Though I started the initiative in 2014, the seed had been sown in my mind long ago. While working in the West Bokaro Division, I used to provide diversity-related training to youth selected from surrounding areas. The training lasted for three months, during which we trained people from a 'diverse background.' The goal was to align them with the values and ecosystem of the organization.

It was this experience that inspired me to begin the skill-based training.

But later, it got stuck in the maze of government policies. Changes happened very frequently, and things were becoming tougher and more complex.

I started realizing that it's one thing to see a vision and begin an initiative with the right intention, and it's an entirely different matter to make it commercially viable. Unless a project becomes commercially viable, it does not progress and grows and dries up. The challenge is – doing things the right way with honesty and goodness when you see others taking shortcuts, and still making it a commercial success.

The government tightens the nuts and bolts of the system to control the majority of people whose focus is just to make money, and they are ready to compromise, lie, and misguide government agencies. In the process, good people who want to do things the right way have to suffer a lot.

I remember, with new policy changes, we were asked by the government to visit Ranchi, the state capital, with physical records of attendance, training, and placement, etc. The condition of roads had never been good in the state of Jharkhand (we are speaking of the year 2014), and it was a regular struggle for us to spend days just traveling instead of making use of digital and online systems, which could easily have been used. But thanks to the twisted characters, who had also encroached into the field of education and skill-building, people like us were struggling and spending a lot of time.

Finally, after investing almost two million of my personal worth, I had to stop the program.

I had a dream to expand our skill-building initiatives to the level of ITI (Industrial Training Institutes) and higher levels of skill-building, and now it was all over.

It gave me deep insight as to why our country's progress is slower than the progress of western countries.

In western countries, people follow rules.

In our country, people are busy finding ways to bypass rules. You can see many easy examples on the streets while driving.

This indeed makes it difficult for those who want to follow rules because the government keeps on applying new rules to curb habitual violators.

It did make it difficult for me, which is why I finally had to stop my pursuit of skill-building somewhere midway.

But as they say, life is all about gaining experiences, and it was one such enriching experience which taught me many aspects of our society and country. Some people still make it a success despite the struggle against the system, and I salute such people.

Whether you succeed or gain some valuable experiences, you are still a winner, either way.

"Whenever possible – and in whichever capacity it's possible – contribute to society. You get enriched in return. You also understand life and the way the world functions better."

CHAPTER FIFTEEN

S-Curves of Life

Life is a strange journey.

When you reflect back, the same seemingly mundane experiences seem to connect to give a picture that we could never see earlier. The earlier moments of joy, pain, and surprises now seem to tell an interconnected story and paint a picture where dots that we could not decipher earlier.

We may call it destiny or 'bhagya ka likha,' but one thing is certain – we can connect the stories only when we look back and reflect. Most of us never look back and reflect, hence the patterns never emerge in our minds. But those who take out some time to reflect, do see the patterns and see life in a better light.

In my experience, writing one's autobiography is one of the best ways to see these connections and patterns. Some people also practice meditation to reflect and understand their life better. There are other ways of reflecting back on our journey.

While writing this book and reflecting on my past experiences, I found that I have been blessed with many opportunities which today appear to be God-sent.

On the other hand, I also went through a sense of loss which again appeared to be planned by destiny.

Now, I can connect the stories which clearly seem to be interrelated.

Without some of these developments – both good or bad – I would never have reached the stage in life where I have.

Let me talk about some of the connections – and toward the end – we shall also talk about some lessons which, hopefully, will be useful for the readers.

Having spent all my childhood days in Jamshedpur, where I saw a great quality of life, I got an opportunity to later bring about improvements in the life of people at West Bokaro. Had I not been in Jamshedpur, I would probably not have felt the experience to make West Bokaro a better place when I got the opportunity to do so.

The love and affection which I received from many seniors helped develop my personality in a more holistic way. Without the support of these people, some of the rough and uncut edges of my personality would not have been smoothed, and I would not have added the value which I think I did. I have mentioned a few such names in this book in various chapters. Well, nobody is perfect and like most of you, I am also on the journey of self-discovery and self-improvement.

I also realize that since I had developed a close association with Tatas while being in Jamshedpur, when I later came to West Bokaro and was disenchanted by the initial unpleasant vibes of loneliness in comparison with Jamshedpur, I still stayed put for a while and did not leave the company and place though I did appear for a few interviews in other groups. Something within me told me – "Awadhesh, don't leave this great group. Look at some of the positives of the company even at this remote location and find a way to make things work. Things will get better if you have some patience."

And I am happy that I did not leave West Bokaro. I first fell in love with the place and later got an opportunity to add more facilities to make people enjoy their work and life at the place even better.

I don't think I would ever have got the kind of quality of life and growth which I later experienced at West Bokaro.

My passion for sports also played an important role in helping me live an energetic life at West Bokaro and win over temporary phases of loneliness.

I remember, in 1985, I had a serious adverse development in my life and career which could have forced me to leave the place, but thanks to my seniors who helped me stay put and face the crisis. It gave me a realization that if you exude courage and maintain a deep relationship with people surrounding you, you can sail through life. That was another incident scripted by God which made me feel that there is a higher force which guides my life, especially in tough times.

I also believe now that training programs which I was nominated for by Tata Steel management in 1991; the Performance Ethics Program (PEP) which I became a part of; and my travel to Australia for three months in a mining research institute – all of these paved a smoother path in my life.

Further opportunities to head the division and do good town planning, putting efforts into making a golf course, setting up a bus stand, arranging street lights, and fixing air conditioners in medical wards, etc., were all interconnected with my previous life experiences in my childhood and growing up years.

I also recall some of the incidents which made me believe that our destiny often plays undecipherable games with us which appear enigmatic and make us feel humbled. Let me cite a few such experiences.

In 1993, I was given the opportunity to visit Germany. I was supposed to visit the country in July/August. All of a sudden, I received the news of the passing away of my sister who was hardly 55. She was suffering from a disease. It came as a shock, and I went to my village to take care of the family and also to break this heartbreaking news to my father. Needless to say, my plan to visit Germany was postponed by a few months and was later rescheduled in October of the same year. I went to my village and gave the sad news of my sister's death to my father, but I never knew that this sad news would hit my father so deeply. He felt shaken, but I did not know then that he was, in fact, uprooted.

In October 1993, I went to Germany and back home in India, my father's condition deteriorated abruptly. I had some idea that my father had taken the death of my sister to his heart but did not know that he had become too weak from within. The tree was uprooted, and he passed away in the village while I was learning the intricacies of new-age mining machinery in Dusseldorf, Germany.

I was not given the message by my family probably because they wanted me to continue my international project without interruption. It was only when I landed at Delhi airport that I was given this news. I took a train from Delhi to Patna and from there, I went to my village to perform the rituals. I did the Puja and had my head shaved. I was stunned to find that despite being the only son, I could not do the last rituals of my father.

These are some of those moments that make you realize how small we are in the overall scheme of life and the universe. I had lost my sister and father in a short span of 3-4 months. These were my closest encounters with death.

Things can change rather alarmingly in life.

Let me change gears now and share a few habits of mine which I think have always played an important role in shaping my life. It is because of some of these habits that I could withstand some of these jolts with strength.

One of my habits is to make new friends wherever I visit. There is an interesting way to do this. I play golf, billiards, or some other sport wherever I go, and these activities always introduce me to new friends. Getting connected with new people gives me a fresh perspective on life and keeps me young in thoughts and deeds. Whether it's a finance expert, a business coach, an author, or any other professional whom I have met, they all have played an important role in my life.

If I have to summarize the secret of my joys and contentment, I will say – it is creating new S-curves in both personal and professional lives every few years, say after every five years. This provides new ways to stay excited and find joy at every step in life.

Many readers might have heard of an S-curve. It is used to show how technological advancements happen. One technology follows an S-curve, after which a new technology takes over, and the sequence goes on and on.

Similarly, one has to keep growing and introducing new S-curves in both personal and professional lives.

Staying busy and surrounding oneself with people is not that difficult, and let me share something on this.

I often visit the USA to spend time with my daughter, son-in-law, and their children.

It's a place where I do not know anyone other than my daughter's family. Normally, for many elderly people like me, such visits are lonely experiences.

But not for me.

On many days of the week in the morning, I go for a walk to a nearby jogging park. Morning walk, exercise, or sports have been a part of my life for as many years as I can think of.

As I go for a walk, I invariably see some other men of Indian origin around my age also coming for their morning routine there. When I sit on a bench for a while and see someone else coming there, I strike up a conversation. That's how I make my first friend, and then as we walk, the other man will also say hello to another friend of his. Now we are three, and that is how I always surround myself with a few jolly fellas.

I think this also has to do with my travel to many countries.

Anyone who has traveled to other countries, especially to the western world, might have experienced this – you are walking on a street or in a park, and anyone who passes by you smiles and wishes you good morning or good evening, depending on the time of day. Normally, Indians find this gesture of smiling at strangers a bit funny. They will mostly sheepishly reply with a forced smile and then giggle with their partners if they are in pairs.

For me, this one cultural thing gave me many new friends.

I often used to stop to talk to someone in case someone smiled and wished me in a park or while sitting on a bench. I made many new friends in any country I went to. Soon, I realized, I had used this simple and unique cultural pattern to my advantage by being with people wherever I went.

I never felt lonely in any country.

There is always a way out of any problem and it all depends on you.

Staying engaged with people, job, assignment, or a newly discovered purpose is the key to a fulfilling life.

Sometime, it is a new job which keeps you engaged for five years. Then you look for a next big jump in career or may be a change of company. Then you learn new skills and become your transformed version. Then you start playing a new game of golf and take a few years to hone this new craft and build new friends. After a few years, you decide to take a longer leave from work and take a trip to foreign countries. Each of these changes is like the beginning of a new S-curve in your life.

As I wrote earlier, it's important to keep discovering and creating new S-curves both in professional and personal domains.

Unfortunately, you will meet many people in life for whom life is like just one or two big S-curves before it ends. Think of a person who joins a company in a position and superannuates from the same position, or may be, he got one promotion and that also was seeing his age and experience and not because he actually upgraded himself. Think of a housewife who decided to suppress her talents all her life and remained a cook and caretaker for her family. I am not undermining the very crucial role which a housewife plays but anyone can surely discover a new meaning in one's life by pursuing one's passion and purpose. There are so many new dimensions in life which people should also look for.

I recall, even while attending serious breakdowns in West Bokaro, I never missed coming to the club in the evening and playing a game of Table Tennis or billiards, feel rejuvenated and go back to be with my team members who were attending the ongoing breakdown related work in the night. On the next day morning, I again used to go for my walk or yoga practices before joining the office. In between, I traveled to new places and learned new sports, etc.

This is what I mean when I say that one should pursue new dimensions in life on day-to-day basis be it a corporate person, a businessman or a housewife.

Similarly, one should also find a new S-curve every few years which means a significant new change in life and career.

I have a few lessons for leading a life of freedom post-retirement:

Financial planning: Without this, you can't lead a happy life after superannuation. Hence, this process should start early.

Health: Though your health has got to be a lifelong pursuit for you, you have to be extra cautious after retirement to stay healthy and take care of your body organs.

Social connection: It's crucial that you maintain social networks to keep yourself emotionally and mentally engaged and happy.

Purpose: Keep discovering a new purpose. There has to be an exciting reason for you to look forward to a new day. Over last few months, my purpose is to write and publish my autobiography. Once it is done, for next few years, my purpose will be to see that the book goes to more places and more people and helps as many people as feasible.

"Never let a dull moment come in your journey of life. Whenever you think things are getting boring, learn a new skill and create a new phase. This is the essence of leading an engaging, successful, and happy life."

CHAPTER SIXTEEN

Learning from Others – A Few Case Studies

I have had the privilege of working with many professionals and everyone taught me something. I learned from good professionals and also from those who committed mistakes. I may not have let everyone know but I received inspiration from many people and kept learning even when they did not know about it. It's true, you can learn a lot from people around us, even from people who some of you may not want to be with.

One of the most important things we can do to be successful is to learn from the mistakes of others. To paraphrase what Nido Qubein, very successful businessman and president of High Point University, told us, "Look at people who are where you don't want to be in life. Figure out what they did and don't do it!"

Here, I would narrate a few stories of mistakes which a few professionals in my knowledge committed. This is with just one goal – to help readers take a leaf out of these and stay successful in their life and work.

Yes, I will also share stories of success in this chapter.

So which story should I tell first?

Let me begin with the story of failure and then will share the stories of success as well.

Ramit (name changed) had great technical knowledge. He was from a well-known Engineering college. He was a great mining engineer who knew how to do mine planning and execution. Because of his functional expertise, he always got very good rating in the annual performance appraisal process. He was good with his team and mining operators used to love him. He was always invited by workers in their team picnics and household celebrations. Workers loved him and he was doing well while earning good increments year after year. He was humble and reached out to support people whenever they needed his help.

Sounds like a fit case of a perfect career progression?

Right?

Wrong.

Things were good in the initial years but later on and Ramit for a few promotions in first few years. Most of these were time – as well as performance – bound as he had joined in a good cadre. But then things started looking different. Ramit did not get any promotion for next few years. One of his colleagues from the same Engineering college and the same batch (let's call him Samar), progressed and got into a senior leadership role but Ramit's career stopped progressing.

So, what went wrong?

It's a very important career lesson which I would like you to reflect on a bit.

Ramit was great at managing and leading at his team members but was not as good at managing his colleagues and managers. He was not a very strong communicator and could not influence upon his peers and leaders, especially on strategic matters. His presentation skills were not as good as that of Samar. He felt a little shy in the presence of senior leaders. You could have left him for hours in the mine with mining workers and he would be happy leading and supervising work but if you left him with a few senior leaders in a strategy or planning war room, he would get uncomfortable. He could not work on his communication and presentation skills and could not get ready for higher positions. Also, he was not expressive enough. You had to see his face and make out whether he was angry or calm.

This was the primary reason the management could not trust him with his ability to stand up to senior leaders coming from Jamshedpur and other locations. Despite wanting to promote him due to his strong technical knowledge, the management could not do so. In our pursuit of getting promoted, we often compare our career graph with that of others but forget to upgrade our skills to be worthier. I can speak of many ex-colleagues who wanted promotions and increments but hardly did much to work on their leadership, communication, and influencing skills. People often neglected even basic improvements such as expanding their vocabulary and improving their English.

As we ascend in the hierarchy of success, there is a shift in the required skill set. We need to constantly be aware of this and keep working on ourselves.

So, what happened to Samar? He excelled at communication and managerial skills and was a natural leader. Leave him in a room full of senior leaders, and he would go around shaking hands and building rapport. He met people, conversed with them to build relationships, and sought assistance when needed. While working in the same mine as Ramit, he always reached out to seniors for support. He excelled in sharing and expressing his needs with peers and leaders and asserted himself effectively. He had an inner drive to keep learning and growing. Though not as strong as Ramit in functional expertise, he swiftly climbed the ladder, eventually moving to a larger company in a bigger city, transitioning into the IT domain. He is now a senior client relations professional at a major IT multinational, has traveled extensively, and holds a key

India head position in one of the verticals. He lives in a sprawling condominium in a large metropolitan city and continues to progress in his life and career.

From Ramit and Samar's story, you can understand the powerful role that leadership and related skills—and the ability to work with senior leaders and peers—can play. Ramit found himself 'caged,' whereas Samar avoided this mistake. For Samar, the sky was the limit for growth and prosperity. Despite excelling in mining operations and planning, Ramit's career did not progress as Samar's did.

Let's now consider a few other professionals.

Sumit (name changed) was a skilled maintenance engineer. I observed him steadily advancing in his career and always found him to be a competent professional. He had strong technical knowledge and effective communication skills, which propelled him up the ladder in maintenance. Eventually, he was transferred to the purchase department.

After this transition, I saw a change in his way of working. He was managing a huge budget. Though the purchase department was never the approving authority for spares and services, they were the initiator of the approval process, and the final approval always used to come from user departments or the head of the purchase department from the city where the corporate office was located. But still, being the initiator, he had certain powers, and it appeared to the management that some of the transactions he was involved in were favoring a certain group of vendors more than others. This way of working came under the scanner of the vigilance department, which reported to higher offices, and soon, he was summoned by the head of the unit for a meeting. Sumit was transferred to another location of the company, probably in a bid to stop some of the practices which were going on in the purchase department. It was either a case of lack of supervision as the head of the purchase department or a case of falling prey to malafide intention. Whatever be the reason, he was transferred only to find that he could not fit in the new location also and had to leave the company after a few months.

From being a successful maintenance professional, with a change in department and powers, he was out of the company, and all of this happened in just a few years. When I look back, it often surprises me to see some of the most efficient and intelligent professionals falling prey to arrogance or unethical behavior. It is important for any professional to respect the chair which one holds and keep its integrity.

Let's take another case.

Sanjeev (name changed) used to report to the head of one of the mining units in the company. He had risen to the position of the deputy of the unit head. His ascendance often used to surprise a few leaders because of his not-so-impressive leadership skills or apparent lack of depth of knowledge. But to admit, at least in the initial years, his career was on a fast track.

Though his manager seemed to be fond of him, it was difficult for other peers or team members to appreciate his growth in the organization knowing his average potential, leadership competencies, and knowledge. They were not that impressed with his way of working.

Once, I was chairing a meeting in which Sanjeev was one of the presenters. I wanted to listen to him with an open mind.

In a few minutes, I started realizing that he was giving a hazy picture while apparently knowing that he was doing so. I could see that the data he was presenting on productivity, cost, and production were not in sync. When I asked him questions on non-gelling of data vis-a-vis the overall performance, his reply was casual and unconvincing. He lacked sincerity, dedication, and a focused approach in comparison with the senior position he was holding in the organization. I suspected some data to be wrong and asked him after the meeting about the accuracy of data. I told him that his data did not seem to be authenticated. He said with a smile – "Sir, let's let it go…" you can understand, it was not a professional reply.

Although the overall performance data was not coherent or appeared satisfactory – and since the management was aware of his approach toward data management – many times he was not considered for growth opportunities in the organization. However, since he was a graduate in the core discipline of mining, he used to threaten to quit the job, and a few times, management appeared to be considerate.

Later on, when he was transferred to other divisions of the organization, he could not reflect the potential and competencies required for a divisional head. Looks like, since the time he was promoted, he could not invest some time and efforts for his personal development as well as that of the organization.

It's just one person who transforms a company or a Country – both positively or negatively.

I remember, he was promoted to lead a different division and this resulted in the gradual loss of shine and aura of the division which had been built carefully and tirelessly by a few previous senior leaders. Mine planning suffered as much as the process of taking land clearances did. He took a safe path and forgot that as a leader, one has to take some courageous actions and be ready for taking lead if things did not go well. That is part and parcel of being in a leadership role. He did not initiate some of the actions of acquiring land for extending the mining work on time. As a result, the management was not left with any other option rather than demolishing all the offices, hostels, and houses in the place before mining the areas beneath these important installations. Today, the mining site has lost its charm. It used to be a place with a soul where families came to play in the clubhouse in the evening and people used to celebrate events together. Officers came to the office and new joiners used to enjoy their stay in the nearby hostel. There was an officers' bungalow where visitors used to stay. There were beautiful roads and bungalows in the area.

Today, there is none of this left. All that one can see is mines, dust, and machines. People travel a long distance every day to come to the site office as they all have shifted away to a distant town.

The subsequent leader had to put in some herculean efforts to bring new technology and drive a tough change management process to try and regain a part of the glory which had been lost.

This is what happens when your focus is misdirected toward just managing up. In my opinion, this is a case of lack of upskilling, managing by power and not following the tenets of leading others and self.

Ranvijay (name changed) was another deputy of mine. He was excellent in mine planning, and seeing his talent, I used to ask him to look after the mine planning area and work with geological. His understanding was good. However, he was not confident in turning efforts into results. He was not exactly a great leader and not great at handling independent charge. I remember, once I went to Australia for three months for an academic program, and Ranvijay was put in charge. After I came back from Australia, I was surprised to see a major part of the mining area being handled rather poorly, and we had to take a long time to bring the layout back to the way we wanted it. In my absence, he had made poor and easy decisions, as maybe he could not convince some other peers to do what was right. His vocabulary was not good, and he also did not put effort into personal development. We used to have a daily morning meeting called the war room in which one needed to lead discussions while challenging people and not allowing wrong explanations to change the direction of the discussion. A leader was supposed to not entertain all kinds of 'stories' and make people do real work and bring results. Ranvijay, as some of you might have guessed by now, was not a strong leader there as well. Whenever I used to go out of West Bokaro for external meetings and presentations, I always used to see the results not being exactly up to the mark, and Ranvijay's lack of leadership skills was partly to do with this. Managing good people is easy, but managing 'clever and naughty fellas' is where the real challenge comes, and that also has got to be an important part of your leadership capability.

One area of strength for Ranvijay was his ability to manage government mining officials. Once I realized some of his strengths, like his ability to build rapport with government mining officials, I started giving him this and other kinds of work which suited him.

Overall, he did a good job over a period of time.

My working experience with Ranvijay taught me important lessons in knowing each of our team members well because that is the only way to use every team member's strength and abilities in the best possible way and make the working experience a 'win-win-win' experience for the employee, leader as well as for the company. A leader must devote time to holding one-to-one meetings with each team member once every month or so and should pay attention to their strengths and the work they love doing. This is the only way for a leader to create a winning team.

There is no point in expecting everyone to be great at everything and then keep on flogging them. You are going to have both 'squirrels' and 'fish' in your team, and if you ask the 'squirrel to swim' and 'fish to climb a tree,' everyone will suffer. Employees will suffer as they would never be happy and productive. The team leader, i.e., you, will suffer as your/team's outcomes will be sub-standard. And yes, your company will suffer for sure.

I have shared these stories without any prejudice against anyone. As I have said right in the beginning, I have learned from everyone, including from those who taught me how not to behave and what not to practice.

These case stories are not exactly about certain individuals; instead, I have taken the liberty to incorporate multiple stories in a few cases and narrated the story using one person's name. Let's focus on the lessons we can take and actions we can initiate to avoid committing the same mistakes.

It's not about people; it's about the issues and learnings.

"We meet many professionals and people in our life. Let's be mentally present to observe them and learn lessons from their lives. People are like walking books, and you can see both patterns – practices which you should learn and habits you should never practice."

CHAPTER SEVENTEEN

Life on the Canvas of Green

Thank you for being there with me as I narrated the story of my journey.

Here is the last bit before we meet again, maybe, over my next book. Yes, we all have many stories within us. It's just that we often do not bother to think through and build on these memories.

Here we shall talk a bit about luck, Karma, and how the dots of our deeds connect at some point in our life. This connection makes us humble and keeps us grounded.

I am a strong believer in the power of doing our duties while learning on the way and making course corrections without bothering too much about luck.

I know many people believe very strongly in luck, and I am not against the belief of people. I respect everyone's faith, and I also know the power of our beliefs and faith.

Just ensure that your beliefs do good for you and do not harm others.

But yes, I have always believed in hard work. Let me narrate a little story around this before we close our conversation through this book.

I remember, I never saw my father doing Puja, etc. My mother used to do Puja, but she also was not so inclined toward it. They believed in Karma Yoga. They believed in God though. I also did not wear rings, etc. My wife used to do Puja, and she had a strong belief in faith. I never tried to weaken her belief. Practicing yoga and meditation, etc., after my 'retirement' (though I do not use this word often. For me, life is about staying engaged with work and people) brought me to a stage where I thought I should have believed more in the power of faith and Karma earlier in my life as well.

I see some of these 'connections' in a better light now. Let me narrate an incident. I was almost a topper in my school and was among the top two students. I remember, we had two months to prepare before the final test in our class ten examination (also known as the board examination). During these two months, one of my uncles asked me to teach other students, probably because I was a good student. I diverted my time to teach others and let them pass. As a result, I could not dedicate enough time to my own studies. All the students from my colony whom I taught passed out in the 2nd or 3rd division. But I got fewer marks than what I could have.

Now how do you look at it? I felt cheated by God. In those days, I thought of an incident from the epic Ramayana. In the epic, it has been elaborated that Ravan had some great qualities but he committed one mistake and that became his undoing. I was thinking that despite studying hard and doing well, because of this one 'mistake' of teaching others and losing focus from my own studies, I had secured lesser marks.

Later, I was selected in Bihar Institute of Technology, Sindri on a merit basis. Had I not got the marks which I had got, I would have lost out on securing a place in the Engineering college. Then I realized that God did help me later in life, maybe, and did not let me fall. Also, I became more confident in my basic subjects while teaching. Teaching, as you know, is a great way to learn. This all helped me in the later part of my studies.

I think good things do come back, maybe later. You may call it Karma, or something else, but always remember – doing good to others has a strange way of helping you later on.

Also, while luck is always playing a role, hard work will create more luck for you, and it's something within our capacity.

So keep working without losing hope and learning lessons on the way.

Do good to others and find time to help those who need it while doing something which is within your capacity.

Success will be yours.

I do hope you have enjoyed reading the story while also picking up some actions which you can take to live a better life and career.

As I mentioned, the key lies in discovering new S-Curves in life.

Playing golf provided me one S-curve, and writing this book became another curve.

Now, giving book-talks and ensuring that the book reaches as many people as feasible provides me another S-curve.

A few youngsters and elderly people alike have started reaching out to me in the last few months seeking guidance on financial planning for a good 'retired' (as I said, there is no word like retirement in my dictionary though) life and other aspects of career, success, and life in general. Maybe, God has started opening a new S-curve for me to meet new people and provide guidance to some of them. I am meeting many people nowadays, especially while playing golf. I will be happy to get in touch with you. It's while being with people that we truly experience the joy of sharing and caring.

I wish you success, joy, peace, and fulfillment in all aspects of your life and career.

It's a Saturday morning. I see the beautiful colors of yellow, orange, and crimson red building on the horizon as I look through the window.

It's time for me to go for another game of golf.

Be in touch.

You can reach me at awadheshojha78@gmail.com.

Stay great, inspired, and engaged.

Keep creating new 'S curves' of life.